Ghost Stories

Real Haunted Hospitals and Mental Asylums

(The Haunted Locations and Paranormal Encounters Bundle)

Stephen Cooper

Published By **Darby Connor**

Stephen Cooper

All Rights Reserved

Ghost Stories: Real Haunted Hospitals and Mental Asylums (The Haunted Locations and Paranormal Encounters Bundle)

ISBN 978-0-9959962-6-7

No part of this guidebook shall be reproduced in any form without permission in writing from the publisher except in the case of brief quotations embodied in critical articles or reviews.

Legal & Disclaimer

The information contained in this book is not designed to replace or take the place of any form of medicine or professional medical advice. The information in this book has been provided for educational & entertainment purposes only.

The information contained in this book has been compiled from sources deemed reliable, and it is accurate to the best of the Author's knowledge; however, the Author cannot guarantee its accuracy and validity and cannot be held liable for any errors or omissions. Changes are periodically made to this book. You must consult your doctor or get professional medical advice before using any of the suggested remedies, techniques, or information in this book.

Upon using the information contained in this book, you agree to hold harmless the Author from and against any damages, costs, and expenses, including any legal fees potentially resulting from the application of any of the information provided by this guide. This disclaimer applies to any damages or injury caused by the use and application, whether directly or indirectly, of any advice or information presented, whether for breach of contract, tort, negligence, personal injury, criminal intent, or under any other cause of action.

You agree to accept all risks of using the information presented inside this book. You need to consult a professional medical practitioner in order to ensure you are both able and healthy enough to participate in this program.

Table Of Contents

Chapter 1: Cimarron Meets Marilyn Monroe 1

Chapter 2: Natalie Wood Can Swim 31

Chapter 3: One Man and 4 Parachutes .. 42

Chapter 4: OJ Don't Stand for "Our Justice" 50

Chapter 5: Amelia Earhart.................... 109

Chapter 6: Little Boy Ghost 121

Chapter 7: Closet Monster 141

Chapter 8: Church Ghost...................... 153

Chapter 9: Coon Hunt 169

Chapter 1: Cimarron Meets Marilyn Monroe

Bodie, California is a old gold mining town that lies in the Bodie Hills, not far from Nevada about 75 miles to the southeast from Lake Tahoe. This 19th century town is now a ghost town. The popular word "ghost town" has generally been accepted for a place that is haunted by ghosts however, it is a location which has been abandoned...or does it?

Bodie At its height at the time of 1880, had an active population of 10,000 which was abandoned by the late 1940s. The town was full of structures made of wood, such as churches, jails the hotel, the bank and a schoolhouse along with stores and houses.

Cimarron Sanchez was a twenty-four year old adventurer who was born and brought up in Dog Town, California, located 14 miles to the west of Bodie.

Cimarron has been a kid who was raised on the tales about Bodie He always had the dream of visiting Bodie one day and checking the place out for his own.

The man didn't know what to expect however, he did have an idea of how there would be various types of structures he'd heard from so many different stories.

He was not expecting to be amazed by what he witnessed.

In truth, no one was ever going to be able to imagine the things he witnessed. And when Cimarron thought to share with anyone the events he witnessed and what he experienced He knew that no one will ever believe him...so the story was kept secret to himself...only keeping a record of the incident in a journal was never his intention to publish until he became alive.

In the end, Cimarron was already considered to be a strange person So he didn't want for more detail for those who were only going to relay his tales which would surely increase his reputation as a reputable nutso.

Dancing Feather, his mother was a half-Yokut Indian who was from his native region of the Little River Region. His father's heritage was an amalgamation of Spanish Panamanian, who escaped the slavery of Spanish colonial rule.

Dancing Feather was his name. Cimarron the name is in Spanish is "wild, untamed". As a child, Cimarron did everything he could imagine to achieve the true possible meaning of his name.

From all indications, Cimarron was a loner and his experiences were usually unique.

It was a hot Saturday in the month of May 2023 when Cimarron decided that it was the perfect day to travel by himself to discover the ruins of Bodie, California.

The sun was reaching its highest point above the horizon East, Cimarron was packing his Bushcraft backpack, containing his essentials that he thought would constitute the essentials he'd have to carry for the day. These included 4 glasses of Arrowhead Mountain Spring water, Cheeze-Its and a Snickers bar, bag of pumpkin seeds and an assortment of fruit roll-ups in mango and pineapple varieties.

Cimarron was enthusiastic to go off, and he embraced his dog, Hannah, a 7-month old golden retriever. Then he promised her he'd see her at the end of the day.

Cimarron put up the dog's door so Hannah could venture out of the backyard fenced when she felt the need arose...and Cimarron didn't have to think about arriving at a specific time in order to allow her leave.

As he jumped into the 2014 VW Transporter bus, Cimarron removed the cap of the first Arrowhead water bottle. He then picked up his pumpkin seeds, which he throw out along the highway CA-270 E...as like he'd be making breadcrumbs. However, who cares?

The drive of 14 miles took 29 minutes when driving at the posted speeds. However, Cimarron reached Bodie in just 15 minutes.

The Wild One liked speed.

Cimarron was driving by the Bodie funeral home and cemetery with red brick near the town's edge which featured a huge monument to the memory of the late President James A. Garfield.

Bodie Boot Hill Bodie Boot Hill was located just outside the city's official cemetery.

One of the first things that struck Cimarron when he sped to Bodie and saw how bleak the place was. One reason for this is because Bodie is a very well-known tourism destination with more than 100,000 visitors annually. Therefore, it was rather unsettling to see not a single individual in the entire area as Cimarron drove into the city's central district of Bodie.

Cimarron Cars were parked in the middle of Main Street by the Miners Union Hall structure, which was the main place of meeting for union members. The building also functioned as an entertainment venue that held events, performances, dances and school recitals...and it was also being the saloon.

Before even opening the door to his car, and the car's window in the open position, he could hear music bursting out of Union Hall. Union Hall.

While he was walking towards the doors that swing open at Union Hall, the musical song he was hearing from a distance was more apparent. The tune is "Happy Birthday", sung in a unique and unique style of the legendary Marilyn Monroe.

"Happy Birthday, Mister President," she exclaimed like only a decibel over the volume of her breath.

The bar stool looking up at Marilyn was JFK as well as the president John Kennedy. To the left of Kennedy were two other men that Cimarron instantly recognized because of the number of times they were played that showed the two men on that date, on November 24, 1963. It was Jack Ruby and Lee Harvey Oswald.

Cimarron was a frequent visitor to Reenactment performances before they were at Reno in the past, and he saw the Elvis performance that he felt was very authentic. He was awed by the way these actors appeared, and he sat in a bar stool so close to the stage that he could clearly see the wrinkles on Jack Ruby's eyes and realized that it was odd that they performed without any audience. He thought that perhaps they were practicing.

Marilyn continued to sing to Jack and then bend her body forward beyond the microphone to highlight her ample cleavage. She would like to be certain Jack could see.

Cimarron couldn't believe the authenticity Marilyn she sounded, and also how she had got the essence of Marilyn.

The first impression that Cimarron had of him was that he'd stumbled upon the rehearsal of some type tribute band was awe inspiring as the group continued to talk and behave with the same mannerisms the characters they played for...as Jack ordered a bowl of chowda, and pulled the cinch tighter on his lower back brace.

Jack was a little flirty with Marilyn when he enticed her to sit down in his lap.

"Come on Norma Jean, you know daddy needs some loving," Jack said.

Marilyn moved to Jack like a snake to its victim.

Marilyn spoke to Jack and he replied, "Do you think Jackie will mind?"

A woman wearing a pillbox hat on the edge of the bar called at the bar "Hell no, you can have that cheating son-of-a bitch."

Jack shouted to his defense saying that he had no intention of doing anything wrong but wanted to offer relief to Marilyn and her family, who appeared to be in a state of distress for her birthday celebration, which was the 29th of May. The year 1917 was the birth date of Jack. Jack will be turning 106.

Cimarron sat enthralled by the chatter between the performers while was seated on a bar stool that was tucked away among sevenstools in front of a magnificent traditional bar from the west in a scene best described as an western saloon.

The saloon could also be referred to as a drinking trough, bughouse shebang or cantina as well as a Gin mill.

Cimarron remembers his great-grandfather sharing tales of his own memories of his favourite saloons in the past.

Saloons during Saloons in the Old West were a central aspect of American Western culture, from tiny towns to larger cities. They were renowned for gambling and drinking and gambling, but they also functioned as a place for socializing.

Contrary to what is depicted in Western films, life in a saloon did not have to be packed with fights and bluffs in the game of poker.

Saloons were just for fun, not shooting competitions.

Living in the American frontier can be thrilling However, it also can be very lonely. After a hard day on the ground construction of railroads, mining, men in their 20s needed some time to relax and wind down. Saloons provided them with a means to get away from the loneliness in the wilderness. Much like us, in the evening, after a hard day's working, they decided to go out to have an evening drink.

This bar resembled a hunting lodge. It was decorated with exquisite work on the wood and a collection of animal heads adorning the walls.

There were numerous chandeliers. And the whole rear of the bar was an enormous cloud-like mirror, surrounded by a dark wooden frame.

As per the set The bartender was an exact replica of Jackie Gleason, larger than life.

"What can I get you pardner," Jackie asked.

"You got any good whiskey?" Cimarron asked.

"Why yes, we do, as a matter of fact," the bartender flashed his signature Gleason smile.

"We have a unique bottle George Roe Ireland Whiskey. The distillery was shut down in 1923. This is a century old vintage. There are only a few open bottles remaining in the world. The most recent auction held of San Francisco a bottle sold at $14,000...but there's a chance that your cash won't be worth it. The bottle is on the property."

"Well thank you, that's very neighbors of you. What should I do? Mr. Gleason?" Cimarron asked as he sipped from the shot glass of rare amber liquid.

"You can just call me 'The Great One '...everyone else does."

While Cimarron began to drink his first swig and felt the whiskey slick through his throat, a man walked up to him as he sat behind the bar appearing to be a stunning representation of Art Carney, and said "You aren't from around here are you, mister."

"Well actually I am, Art," Cimarron responded trying to integrate himself in what he believed was a play that was invited to participate in.

While Cimarron sipped the last of this unique whiskey the man looked up and saw Marilyn telling him, with a smile, that he must come back.

Cimarron was not afraid to jump to her feet to celebrate And, following the hand signals of Marilyn, joined her on the chaise lounge, where she relaxed in her perfect Marilyn posture.

"Hello, big boy, what's your name," Marilyn exclaimed.

"My name is Cimarron."

"Well, that's a proper name for a cowboy, I guess," Marilyn smiled when she reached her hand out to kiss Cimarron in the back. It was a bit odd that he did not feel anything however he thought the best of it. He thought the whiskey might have resulted in a feeling of numbness.

Then, JFK popped up, obviously irritated by the advances of Marilyn as he walked over to the bar for a second shot of his most-loved drink that is the Bloody Mary.

"What brings you to these parts?" Marilyn inquired.

"Oh, I'm just adventure hunting, I guess you'd say."

"Should I call you Marilyn or Norma Jean?"

"Well, since I hardly know you, I guess you can call me Marilyn, but maybe by the end of the night you can call me Norma Jean," Marilyn smiled.

Cimarron said, "This is quite an group you have come up with. What are you going to be touring...Vegas, Reno?"

Marilyn's response was laughter and then, with a frown and asked him what he thought he was thinking about when he said that they could stage an event somewhere.

Cimarron insists that he believed their personalities are spot on and people were going to be blown away.

And then, Marilyn just stopped and looked at Cimarron.

"What are you referring to by "characters?"

"You know, the resemblance each of you have to the original characters you are pretending to be."

Marilyn stopped for a lengthy period of time, then turned towards Cimarron and stated "You do not believe there's any truth to us, do you?

"Well no, of course there's no way. There's not been that many drinks of whiskey."

"Well, what if I told you what nobody knows about how I passed...then would you believe?"

Cimarron considered this to be a great element of the game which he found himself in So he said "Sure."

Marilyn said, "They say that I passed away from an overdose of sleeping pills. The report by the coroner's toxicology department declared that the reason for death was acute poisoning with barbiturate and eliminated the possibility of it being accidental because the doses exceeded the limit of lethal.

Marilyn continued...however the rumors nearly instantly surfaced suggesting there was foul play involved. Those persist throughout these decades, all the way to today.

In 1982 The Los Angeles County District Attorney's office started investigating whether there was sufficient evidence for an investigation on my death. However, they could not discover any evidence that could back the claim that I had been murdered.

Ha! They like what you consider, Marilyn expressed with a an angry smile.

Marilyn continued to recount the full story: "At 3:30am on August 5th 1962 my psychiatrist doctor, Dr. Ralph Greenson, broke into my bedroom, smashing the window and found me dead on my bedroom, and an empty sleeping pill bottle placed on my nightstand.

The housekeeper of my home, Eunice Murray been awakened during the night to discover the lights on my bedroom and the door unlocked. Murray phoned the doctor Dr. Greenson, worried that there was something wrong.

The issue with the well-known claim that I died from an overdose that I self-inflicted is there's conflicting evidence by my press relations supervisor, Arthur Jacobs, that contests the timeline that was claimed to be my demise.

At around 10:30 pm on August 4 An attendant informed Jacobs that there was something terribly off at the Hollywood bowl. This was clearly far earlier than the much reported 3:30am finding of my body. "That's false, since my husband was also there. My husband was able to fudge everything," Jacobs's wife has since stated in testimony. However, a number of members from the ambulance crew are claiming that I'd actually been brought to the hospital in an ambulance that night, still alive. I was killed on the way for the hospital.

Robert Kennedy was at my home at the end of afternoon on my death day.

The thought of sitting next to Marilyn, Robert Kennedy, or his twin looked at him with a smile.

The days prior to my passing in the days leading up to my death, I was "very much in love and was going to marry Bobby Kennedy."

Bobby and me fought to the death that day before my demise.

It's not talked about However, Kennedy took off to the airport by helicopter in order to board a plane at around 2 or 3 am in the evening of my demise.

In a flash, at the very edge of the bar Joe DiMaggio's ghost popped up to speak above Marilyn's protest.

DiMaggio was devoted to his former wife so deeply so much that the man never repaid his acquaintance Frank Sinatra for introducing her to the Kennedy family.

Marilyn added "I was coping with depression and drug addiction around the time rumors about affairs with John F. Kennedy and Bobby Kennedy began circulating."

DiMaggio interrupted, "The understanding was that her involvement with Mr. Sinatra and the Kennedy clan put her in a position where maybe it wasn't good for her mental health or her emotional health."

DiMaggio complained, "I didn't think they were good people for her to be around."

Marilyn's suicide at the age of 36 on the 5th of August 1962, just 17 month following her treatment for psychiatric disorders, was declared as a "probable suicide. It was my belief that somebody would "do her in,"" Joe declared with a firm slam of his hand at the bar.

"'The whole lot of Kennedys were lady-killers, and they always got away with it.

They'll be getting away with it a hundred years from now.'"

"I always knew who killed her, but I didn't want to start a revolution in this country," DiMaggio stated.

"I went to my grave regretting and blaming myself for what happened to her."

I'm the person who was the one who loved Marilyn all the way to the final. I was the one who brought flowers for Marilyn's Los Angeles grave until my passing away in the year 1999. When I was dying, I declared "I'll finally get to see Marilyn...and here I am."

He stated that Monroe was killed by the CIA in connection with her relationship to Robert F. Kennedy, since the agency was seeking revenge on the Kennedys' actions in The Bay of Pigs.

And then, "Old "Blue Eyes", Frank Sinatra appeared in the crowd gathering in the vicinity of Joe, Marilyn and Cimarron.

Frank commented, "The weekend before her passing away, Marilyn spent time at the renowned Cal Neva Lodge, outside of Lake Tahoe, which I part-owned.

The only thing that the public didn't know about her was that she had come to visit her former husband Joe DiMaggio who was staying near by, and she made a public announcement in the week following about their return together.

The announcement of a press event sparked speculation that Marilyn was planning to reveal the details of her relations with JFK as well as RFK.

Yet, Frank said, " she'd never have spilled about the Kennedys because she still had feelings for Jack."

And Frank said, "if the press conference was not scheduled, she could have lived for a long time.

After Marilyn's death the attorney I worked with, Mickey Rudin, who also was a co-worker alongside Marilyn I was told that she was executed. There was also a rumor in circulation among Mob boss Sam Giancana's gang, some who claimed to be involved."

"I have several sources that have told me the exact same story, Frank said: "She'd been killed using an Nembutal Suppository, as well as Robert Kennedy or the Mob was involved."

DiMaggio was the one who arranged Monroe's funeral and over the following 20 years, had white flowers dropped at her tomb twice each week, had no desire to speak publicly about what he thought transpired. But, he endorsed the release of his memoirs shortly after his passing.

"The Yankee Clipper, as he was called, claimed to have read Hollywood actress's diary following her passing."

The diary of Monroe vanished shortly after however, as per DiMaggio: "Marilyn had apparently noted her conversations with Robert Kennedy about CIA plans to poison Fidel Castro with the aid of the Chicago gangster Sam Giancana, and the government's investigation into union leader Jimmy Hoffa's Mafia links."

Joe stated, "Marilyn met the Kennedys through Peter Lawford, their British brother-in-law, and is believed to have passed on Robert's pillow talk to Frank Sinatra, who in turn reported to Giancana."

Joe told his story about how Marilyn addressed Joe Jr., his son Joe Jr at the night of her death, telling him she was determined to set the record straight.

"She said she spoke with RFK [Robert Kennedy] three or four times a week and he told her about the work he was doing," Joe said. "He mentioned which mobsters they were going after. Marilyn would pass on some of those tidbits to Sinatra, according to Joe Jr."

DiMaggio acknowledged that he cried none of his tears after the Kennedys were shot dead.

"I believed they got what they deserved," Joe declared with a happy smile.

John and Bobby who were sitting one arm's distance away each one slouching on the chair after hearing Joe's comment.

Jackie Gleason piped in from behind the bar "DiMaggio was 84 years old when passed away after a prolonged fight against cancer.He was unable to shake Robert Kennedy's hands when they came together at the New York's Yankee Stadium. A few years prior to the time the time he passed away, he promised to attend Kennedy Centre. Kennedy Centre only if no person from the circle of political families was present."

"JFK killed my Marilyn, plain and simple...and you can say you heard it from an indisputable source," Joe declared.

Marilyn just smiled at Joe after which she turned her attention to JFK and Bobby She said "The reality is, I've never lied to anyone. It's been a while since I let people get themselves into trouble."

Cimarron stood there for a while, thinking about what Marilyn and Joe were saying, and pondering that there were some details regarding Marilyn's passing that he'd not heard of confirmed with this conviction or direct witness.

Marilyn told me that from where she was she was, she'd accepted their apology for the trespasses they had committed And that was the end of it.

More shockingly than Cimarron considering Joe DiMaggio's assertions Marilyn left from the same hand as JFK.

Jack Ruby and Lee Harvey were right behind them and it was apparent that there wasn't any conflict between them. JFK...in the actual fact, when they were chatting, JFK flatly repeated what they were all aware of...

It was not Lyndon Johnson who had JFK murdered. This wasn't even either the Mob or the huge army industrial complex.

Kennedy looked at his watch, but no, the answer wasn't one among those...it it was CIA.

Kennedy confessed to being frustrated by the heinous actions of the CIA pulled. He discovered that the CIA wanted to assassinate Cuban president Fidel Castro. Thus, it was widely known about the CIA believed Kennedy would be the one to break up their organization. Because of this it was they that ordered the execution of Kennedy.

Jack was adamant, "Poor Ruby and Oswald. They were just"fall guys" that the CIA created to hide their bases."

Ruby and Oswald turned to Jack with thoughtful smiles, as they raised their arms toward the sky as if they said, "oh well."

In JFK's colossal declaration, Marilyn, Joe, the Kennedy's, and Sinatra were all gone amid smoke clouds.

They were actors or perhaps physical images that were that were sent through Cimarron through Pixar?

Is there a magician hiding behind a curtain that was that was directing the play?

Did Cimarron experiencing the full benefits of Irish whiskey?

Cimarron was skeptical of ghosts. But these spirits convinced him to reconsider his belief.

Cimarron was gobsmacked, however it wasn't for long...as Natalie Wood came through the saloon's swinging doors.

Chapter 2: Natalie Wood Can Swim

Natalie Wood strutted into the saloon, dressed to the nines with her famous gown from her film role in Gypsy.

She was prettier than Cimarron was in films as Splendor in the Grass or West Side Story.

Cimarron was aware she knew that Natalie Wood was an American actress who was drowned in a boat along with husband Robert Wagner and friend Christopher Walken off Catalina Island in Southern California.

Natalie's death has been a mystery for a long time. Robert Wagner was an early suspect in the Natalie's death.

in 2022 Wagner had his case cleared, as Natalie Wood's trial was declared cold. There are a variety of theories regarding the incident that took place, however, nobody is sure...except obviously,

Natalie...and possibly anyone who was present to witness her drown.

Natalie took a seat and instructed Jackie Gleason to come over.

Jackie smiled and then with an eagle's grin declared "And away we go!"

Jackie was able to glide across to Natalie and asked, "What will it be my dear."

"Hi, Jackie. It's nice to meet you out and around. Would you be able to offer me a glass of Pouilly-Fuisse."

Jackie returned quickly, with Natalie's drink on the other, with her favorite flowers, the gardenia with a vase in the other.

Natalie looked at Cimarron and replied, "Marilyn told me I could find you here. They said that you'd be the only one to eventually find the truth about what really happened for us."

Cimarron was shocked at this comment, and he told Natalie that he wasn't sure as to what his job was within this context, or whether this really was true.

Natalie told him this was indeed true Natalie was certain that it was real, and she longed for Cimarron to share with everyone about what transpired to her that night that she passed away.

"In November of 1981, myself along with my spouse Robert Wagner, and actor Christopher Walken went on a boat cruise on Catalina Island, along with Captain Dennis Davern.

The night of November 28th We all ate dinner at a local restaurant in Catalina and enjoyed a couple of drinks prior to returning to the yacht. According to my husband I went to our cabin for a nap in the early hours of 10:45 p.m. While he was speaking to Walken. My husband came back to the cabin afterward and told the police that I had gone not there.

The man claimed to have searched on the boat and realized that the dinghy had disappeared and the dinghy was also gone, as reported by Town and Country Magazine. In the aftermath, Harbor Patrol and Coast Guard were notified of the incident within a couple of hours the body of my floating was located.

I died on November 29 around 7:44 a.m.

There remain controversies regarding the causes that led to my demise. At the time it was believed to be accidental, however people speculated that there was some more truth to the tale.

One of them was that my sister has rightly argued that I don't swim to the sea with a dinghy because I'm terrified of the water. I would never take a dip in my swimming pool.

RJ The nickname we used to call him. He said he thought that I might have had difficulty sleeping because of the Dinghy always hitting the boat and I may be sat up trying to tie it up and plunged into the sea. Some, however, believe the involvement of foul play.

The coroner had officially determined my death was an accident, and in my death certificate"a "probable drowning in the ocean."

In 2011 in 2011, it was reported that the Los Angeles County Sheriff's Department opened an investigation on my unsolved death. Since then, additional details have come to light and a person has stated that Christopher Walken may have witnessed me as well as RJ fighting in the night.

Additionally, assistance wasn't immediately contacted after RJ states that he found out I had gone missing.

It wasn't until several hours later that the incident was first reported. Witnesses from the new witnesses -- several people on their own vessels during the time have also come forward to say they heard shouting as well as a woman yelling to get help during that fateful night. This, of course, was my experience.

These evidences suggests that my death could not be a simple drowning accident.

In the event that my investigation into my death was revisited, the cause for my demise was changed from "undetermined." My body was discovered in my bed clothes -an flannel, plaid nightgown and socks made of argyle, as well as a red down jacket. According to The Daily Mail, my blood alcohol level was 0.14 percent, which was above the legal limit of 0.14.

Certain drugs -- primarily for motion sickness and painare also present within my bloodstream. This isn't too shocking considering that I had been recognized to have drunk the alcohol when I had dinner with my friends.

There were injuries that appeared on various areas of my body, including knees, ankles, and wrists.

In the report of 1981, the bruises were explained as a result of me hitting my body against the yacht's side when I tried to get up having fallen over.

The coroner's report following the reinvestigation says that the bruising occurred prior to my entry in the water. "The location of the bruises, the multiplicity of the bruises, lack of head trauma, or facial bruising support bruising having occurred prior to entry in the water," the latest report says.

Furthermore, the boat's skipper, Dennis Davern, revealed during his interview that he had lied in his police interview. If asked if he believed my beloved husband, RJ, was responsible He replied "Yes, I would say so. Yes."

While I've changed the cause of my death to "undetermined," there is nothing to prove my bruises or what happened that night I died. death...but we're here to reveal what happened to me when I passed away.

Simple and straightforward, RJ and I had an intense fight on the night. We had both consumed a lot of drinks and RJ became obsessed by jealousy and thought I was being too romantic with Chris.

The argument grew heated in the living room. I then took a walk onto the deck to avoid RJ however, he stayed with me.

The screaming continued until I was exhausted and began to strike RJ. This was all it took to get RJ to respond, and boy did it. He grabbed me with his wrists, and then tossed me around as if I was a rag doll on the deck. There, I smashed my knees and ankles very hard.

After I woke up, I confronted with him only to see him react by pushing me forward. I was just too close to the boat's edge which caused me to fall over into the sea.

Contrary to the reports of some I did swim if I needed to. However, the time came that I smashed my head into the dinghy, and fell unconscious.

Before I could call "help" I was underwater and I was unable to find my way back.

I'd like to believe RJ was seeking me and tried to help me however, like I said I was knocked unconscious.

It's sad to say that the stories I've heard from this past life about the way RJ believes I drowned myself make us wish to see him in the future in the near future, which is likely to not take as lengthy. You know, he's 93.

It's a bit of a mystery there's no way that he deliberately killed me. The incident is an accident...but I certainly wish I had known about the fact that I had been with a drunken condition all on my own and his hands were spotless.

It seems like he did not wish to be faced with an audience and trial in which he might be found guilty of involuntary manslaughter.

My sibling Lana is aware of the truth regarding RJ and has told anybody who's willing to listen.

We were married twice but it's not going to be a 3rd time.

According to Ricky Arnez always says, "He'll have a lot of splaining to do."

And with that Natalie was up, she stood and looked at Cimarron for the last time "Tell Bud that I'm waiting for him, won't you?"

Cimarron's fondness for the old films allowed him to draw a link to Natalie's connection. The actress was speaking of the love that she had in her heart' Bud Stamper, played by Warren Beatty in Splendor in the grass.

After that, Natalie left through the swinging doors to the tavern, and left Cimarron to be alone in his thoughts and awe.

Chapter 3: One Man and 4 Parachutes

In the solitude, Cimarron was surprised that the person who came through the saloon's swinging doors did not look like someone was not his acquaintance as an a-lister.

"My moniker is Jack Polack, alias Dan Cooper You may recognize me as D.B. Cooper...the name given by the media to me.

I love air pirates," the man said while he sat on the bar stool and placed an order for the Anchor Steam Beer.

Jackie always snuck up quick to slide D.B. the drink.

Jack Polack explained, "D.B. Cooper is the epithet of media I was pinched with as the man unidentified who pried off Northwest Orient Airlines Flight 305 which was a Boeing 727 airplane, inside United States airspace on November 24 November, 1971.

When I flew between Portland, Oregon to Seattle, Washington, I told an airline attendant that I was carrying bombs, and demanded an amount of ransom in the range of $200,000 which would be roughly $1,400,000 by 2023 I also requested the use of four parachutes when I landed in Seattle.

Following the release of passengers from Seattle after which I directed the crew of the flight to refill the aircraft before launching another flight towards Mexico City, with a stopping for refueling within Reno, Nevada. After about 30 minutes of the departure from Seattle I stepped through the door to the plane's rear and lowered the stairs and then parachuted off into night in the Southwest of Washington. The location of my disappearance was not clearly located.

In the year 1980, a little part of the ransom cash was located in the waters of the Columbia River. The finding of the ransom money brought renewed interest to the case, but it did not provide more information on my fate or identity as the rest of the money wasn't ever recovered.

I declared myself to be Dan Cooper, but a journalist mistook my name for an unidentified suspect, and I changed my name to "D. B. Cooper".

In the 45 years following the hijacking incident, it was the Federal Bureau of Investigation maintained an active investigation and constructed an extensive file of cases however, they were unable to arrive at any conclusive conclusions.

It remains the one and only mystery of pirated airspace in the past of aviation commercial. The FBI suggests that I could not make it through the leap because of a number of factors: the weather conditions that were insurmountable on the evening of the hijacking, my inexperience with equipment for skydiving, the densely forested area in which I plunged and my lack of specific information about the landing site and also the disappearance the ransom amount, which suggests that it wasn't used.

In July of this year The FBI had officially suspended the active investigations into the NORJAK (Northwest hijacking) investigation, even though reporters and enthusiasts, professionals as well as amateur sleuths continue to investigate a myriad of theories about my identity, fate as well as fate.

My hijacking, along with several others later on in the year that followed--led to a major change in the rules of commercial aviation as well as stricter security measures for airports. Metal detectors were put in place as well as baggage inspection became a mandatory requirement passengers who had bought tickets with cash on departure day were screened for further scrutiny.

Boeing 727s were upgraded with the eponymous "Cooper vanes", specifically created to stop the forward stairs from falling down during flight. In 1973, hijackings had declined, due to the security improvements that effectively deterred potential hijackers whose primary motive was financial gain.

We're here to inform you that I managed to succeed in landing. The drop zone actually was to the south-southeast of my initial estimation, and was located in the drainage region in the Washougal River.

An eruption in 1980 of Mount St Helens obliterated any remains of the physical evidence I had left from my arrival.

I left eight Raleigh cigarettes with filters within the ashtray in my armrest that was the FBI might have utilized to detect DNA. However, they couldn't identify fingerprints. Therefore, they later returned the butts the Las Vegas field office, that was then inexplicably destroyed.

I chose a seat on the final row of the cabin in the rear for three motives: to be able to watch and take action to whatever is happening that was happening in front of me, to limit the risk of being confronted and attacked by one in front of me, and also to keep myself from being noticed by other passengers.

To make sure I would not receive sabotage equipment, I requested four parachutes so that I could force an assumption that I would be able to force any hostages I could get to join me in my jump.

FBI Agent Ralph Himmelsbach noted my choice for a bomb, instead of the other weapons used previously by hijackers-- crucified any attempt to hurry me.

Also, I made sure to not leave any evidence. When I was about to jump into the air, I requested that the flight attendant Mucklow give me back any notes that were written by me or on my behalf. Mucklow claimed she had utilized the match from my matchbook on paper to ignite the cigarettes of one of me after which she resisted attempts to get rid of my matchbook empty I demanded that she return the matchbook to me.

While I took my time in my efforts to find evidence, I did not succeed and I was unable to find my tie clip at my desk. The mistake proved to be that it was not a contributing factor to bringing the FBI towards me or my identification.

In November of 1976 in November 1976, a Portland grand jury issued an indictment of absentia in the case of "John Doe, a.k.a. Dan Cooper" for pirated airspace and a violation of the Hobbs Act. The indictment was officially launched a legal proceedings that will continue should the hijacker be arrested anytime in the near future.

They could take the indictment they received and put it in a place where sun does not shine.

They won't imprison me since I'm dead. The money I did not spend is stashed into a safe place is likely to be searched for a long time from now...but won't locate.

That's why you should tell the smart FBI people that I survived. I had a great time living within Elmer City, Washington, running a fuel station, and enjoying a tranquil lifestyle.

Chapter 4: OJ Don't Stand for "Our Justice"

Cimarron did not recognize the couple who walked through the doors of the saloon swinging following, on the basis of numerous video stories he watched as a child, which covered the deaths of the couple as well as the suspected murderer, OJ Simpson. The couple's death predated his birth by five years.

Ron Goldman and Nicole Brown Simpson Nicole Brown Simpson, the ex-wife of OJ, were slain, murdered, and then brutally stabbed outside Nicole Simpson's home located in the Brentwood neighborhood in Los Angeles, on the 12th of June the 12th of June, 1994.

Ghosts from the past were known for their famous figure believed as the killer...Orenthal James Simpson.

OJ Simpson, who is famous for his professional and college football teams, and also for his film and television acting He was arrested as the suspect in their murder and brought to trial. The trial lasted 11 months, from November 1994 until October of 1995.

Nicole was walking towards Cimarron, and she said, "We heard that you're the guy who is going to help us get the truth out about what happened to Ron and me." After that she wrote down an account in the newspaper of their deaths and the trials.

Cimarron was still drinking the whiskey before saying "Thanks. I'm not sure of what you'd like me to accomplish," and proceeded to go through the article in the paper.

He read aloud the following sentence: Although prosecutors claimed they believed Simpson was implicated in an extensive amount of evidence from forensics, Simpson was acquitted on all murder charges on the 3rd of October, 1995. The trial was held just after the Los Angeles protests. Many commentators believe that the defense benefited from the anger of Los Angeles' African American Community toward the LAPD who was known for its racism, and convinced jurors of majority Blacks to convict Simpson. The trial is usually referred to as the "trial of century" due to due to its global media coverage as well as being said to be one of the "most publicized" criminal trial throughout human history.

In the wake of police investigations, Simpson was formally charged for the murders on the 17th of June, after police discovered a glove stained with blood on the property of Simpson.

When he failed to submit himself to the time he was scheduled, he was the target of a pursuit at low speed with the white 1993 Ford Bronco SUV owned and driven by his buddy Al Cowings.

Television networks interrupted the broadcasts during 1994's NBA Finals to broadcast live broadcasts of the pursuit that was watched by around 95 million viewers. The chase and the arrest of Simpson following the same day, are some of the most popular moments in American the history of television.

The trial was seen as historic due to the broad divide over this verdict among the people. The opinions of observers about the verdict was influenced by their ethnicity. The media described this as"the "racial gap".

An online survey among Los Angeles County residents showed that the majority

African Americans thought that the "not guilty" verdict was legitimate, whereas the majority of whites believed the verdict was motivated by race. juror nullification by a majority African American jury.

The latest polls indicate that the "gap" has narrowed since the trial.

More than half of black respondents polled said they believed that Simpson had been guilty.

In the night on June 12 on the 12th of June, 1994 Brown and Simpson were both present at their daughter Sydney's dance performance in Paul Revere Middle School. After the show, Brown and her family had dinner at Mezzaluna restaurant. They didn't invite Simpson to accompany them.

One of the servers in the restaurant were Ron Goldman, who had became close to Brown over the past few weeks however wasn't assigned to his place at the Brown the family's dining table. Brown along with her kids visited Ben and Jerry's restaurant before returning to her home located in Bundy, Brentwood.

Manager of Mezzaluna told the story of how Brown's mother called the restaurant on 9:37pm about the loss of a pair of eyeglasses. The manager retrieved the glasses and placed them inside the envelope in white. Goldman carried with him when leaving the restaurant at the conclusion of his shift, at 9:50 pm. He planned to take it home at Brown's home.

While in the meantime, Simpson ate takeout food at McDonald's along with Kato Kaelin. She was a part-time actor and a friend of the family who was given access to the Simpson's guest house estate. The rumor mill was abuzz that Simpson was a drug user during the time of the murder. The newspaper's Cindy

Adams reported that the couple had been to an area Burger King, where a well-known drug dealer identified only by the name of "J. R." was convicted of selling the pair crystal meth.

Brown's neighbors claimed to have saw barking and screams coming out of the outside all evening, starting about 10:15 am.

About 10:55 p.m. An animal walker who was a couple of blocks from Brown was able to spot Brown's Akita dog, who was barking on the road outside her house. The Akita who's legs were stained with blood, accompanied the man back home. He tried walking back the animal to where he saw it however, the dog refused.

After that, he walked away the Akita to a couple, who agreed to take the dog for a night; however, as the dog became agitated, the owners decided to return it to the place it was found.

At midnight, when they walked towards the location that the Akita was found when the dog walked out of Brown's house and they saw Brown's corpse lying in the front of the home. The police were dispatched to the scene, and discovered Goldman's remains in the vicinity of Brown's.

The entrance to Brown's residence was opened at the time of discovery There were however no indications of anyone having got into the apartment, either via a breach or any other method.

Brown's body lay on her back, barefoot and lying in the middle of the steps leading to the entrance. The pathway connecting to the stairs was covered in blood but Brown's shoes were spotless Based on the evidence, the investigators determined that she was the very first to be murdered and was the target of choice.

Her body was repeatedly stabbed times on the neck and head, however there were not many wounds of defense on her hands, which suggested that it was a brief struggle for detectives. The wound that was inflicted to her neck ran through her neck and cut the carotid artery.

A huge laceration at the middle of her back, with an identical footprint of her feet on her clothes indicated to the investigators that after killing Goldman the killer returned to her body, sat upon her bed, dragged her head back with hair, and cut her throat. The larynx was visible through the gaping cut on her neck. the vertebra C3 was cut Brown's head was barely attached with her body.

Goldman's body was found near the fence and a tree. Goldman was stabbed several times on the neck and the body, but there were a few defense cuts on his hands suggesting a quick struggle to detectives.

The evidence of the Los Angeles County Coroner alleged that the suspect struck Goldman with a single hand as he held Goldman in the chokehold.

On the body of Goldman was an ablue knit cap a left-hand Aris Isotoner lighter leather glove; as well as the envelope with the glasses were returned by him.

The police have determined that Goldman visited Nicole's residence in the time of her murder and Goldman was killed by the murderer in order to disarm Goldman and disperse any witnesses.

The trail of assailant's shoe prints that were bloody slid across the back entrance. The left-hand side prints, there were traces of blood of the attacker and he was bleeding from the left side of his hand.

Comparing the distance between prints showed that the suspect was walking - not running off and away from the location.

In the evening of the 12th of June, Simpson was scheduled to take a red-eye flight to Los Angeles International Airport to Chicago in the United States, where he was scheduled to play golf on the next day during an event with the representatives of Hertz rental automobile Corporation who Simpson was the spokesperson. The plane was scheduled to depart at 11:45 pm when a limousine rolled up to Simpson's Rockingham estate, to take him to the airport at 10:25 at night.

The chauffeur drove the limousine around the estate in order to make sure that he would be able to maneuver the surrounding area in the stretch limousine correctly and also find out which road would offer the most convenient access to the limousine.

He started to ring the intercom around 10:40 and receiving no response. The house appeared dark, and that nobody seemed to be at home. He took a smoke and repeatedly called his boss in order to obtain Simpson's house phone number. The witness testified that at some moment he observed a person identical to Simpson to enter the home via the front door. From there, the driveway begins, but prior to the light switch turning to life.

He didn't know the direction this figure was looking from. The witness testified that he noticed Simpson's house's numbers on the sidewalk near the estate, but that no vehicle was visible.

The prosecution has presented evidence that shows the location near the house's address along the curb, where Simpson's Ford Bronco was found the following day, suggesting that the driver of the limousine likely noticed the Bronco in the event that it was in the area when he came to collect Simpson off.

At the moment the driver of the limousine saw the "shadowy figure" head towards the southern walkway, which is which is where the glove that was bloody would eventually be discovered, Kato Kaelin was having an online chat with a friend.

About 10:40 am At around 10:40, an object crashed against the wall of the guesthouse Kaelin was in, the incident he described as having three "thumps" and which he thought could be an earthquake.

Kaelin left the call and walked out to look into the sounds, but he didn't go straight into the dark, south-facing pathway that the loud thumps started. Instead, he strolled across the building, and noticed the vehicle parked.

Kaelin allowed the limousine to enter after which Simpson was finally able to exit through the front door minutes later. He said that he'd overslept. The limousine driver as well as Kaelin were later to testify that Simpson appeared to be agitated the entire night.

The chauffeur in the limousine noted that as they drove to the airport Simpson was complaining about the heat sweating, then was rolling down the window regardless of it being an extremely hot night. Driver also admitted that he stuffed four bags of luggage bags in the vehicle the night before, with among them was an knapsack Simpson refused to handle, and demanded that he unload the bag himself.

An airport porter said that Simpson went through only three bags in the evening The police later determined that the luggage missing was the same one that the driver of the limousine had previously mentioned.

A witness who was not included in the trial said he witnessed Simpson at the airport throwing objects from a bag to a garbage can.

Investigators Tom Lange and Philip Vannatter think this is the way in which the weapon used in the murder, as well as shoes and clothing that Simpson were wearing during the crime were destroyed.

Simpson was late, but he made it to his destination. The passenger as well as the pilot's testimony revealed that they did not notice any injuries or cuts on the hands of Simpson. Broken glass, a piece of paper with a phone number and bedsheets with blood were taken from the room of Simpson in O'Hare Plaza Hotel. O'Hare Plaza Hotel. The hotel's manager remembered Simpson seeking a band-aid to his ring finger on the reception desk since he "cut it on pieces of note paper".

When he learned that Brown was the victim's female, LAPD commander Keith Bushey instructed officers Tom Lange, Philip Vannatter, Ron Phillips, and Mark Fuhrman to notify Simpson of her demise and transport Simpson to the police station for the collection of their children from the previous couple who were in the apartment of Brown during the killings.

The police rang the intercom in Simpson's home for nearly thirty minutes, but they did not receive a answer. They observed that Simpson's vehicle was set at a sloping point, and its rear side extending further than its front. They also noted that there appeared to be blood on the door that they were concerned the insiders could be injured. Vannatter directed Fuhrman to climb the wall, and then open the gate, allowing three other detectives to access the area.

The police would say that they were able to enter without an warrant of search due to the urgency of the situation, and specifically because of fear that someone may be injured.

Fuhrman briefly spoke with Kaelin and she told investigators that the vehicle was the property of Simpson and earlier in the evening, he'd noticed thumps in his walls. While walking around the area to check what might have led to the noises, Fuhrman found a bloody right-hand glove that was later determined to be the identical pair of the left-hand glove located near the corpse of Goldman. The findings were determined to be sufficient for the issuance of an arrest warrant for Simpson.

Phillips said that the moment he phoned Simpson at the time in Chicago to inform him about Brown's death, Simpson sounded "very upset" but seemed to be unaffected over the cause of the death of her. Phillips pointed out that Simpson did not ask if the kids had witnessed Brown's corpse or the scene of her murder however, she was not worried about what the assailant(s) have hurt children in any way. The police called Simpson at his residence on the 13th of June and brought the man into Parker Center for questioning.

Lange observed Lange noticed that Simpson was suffering from a cut on the left hand, which was in line with the area where the killer was bleeding Then he Lange asked Simpson what he did to get the wound.

In the beginning, Simpson claimed he cut his finger in Chicago when he learned that Brown had died. Lange was then able to inform Simpson that there was blood within his car. At the time, Simpson admitted that he was able to cut his finger the 12th of June, but claimed it was unclear how. Simpson voluntarily donated the blood of his family members for a comparison to evidence that was collected at the scene of the crime and was later released. In June of this year, Simpson hired lawyer Robert Shapiro and began to put together Simpson's legal team (referred to as "The Dream Team"). Shapiro said that a unhappy Simpson was beginning treatment for depression.

Following days the preliminary results of tests on DNA came back with match to Simpson However, the District Attorney waited to file charges until the full tests had been completed. Simpson had a night of rest between June 16-17 in his San Fernando Valley home of the friend of Robert Kardashian. Shapiro requested that several medical professionals examine Simpson's mental health.

On the 17th of June, investigators suggested that Simpson be accused of two murder counts in the first degree and a special case of multiple murders following the last DNA tests were completed. The LAPD advised Shapiro around 8:30 am that Simpson was required to surrender his back that morning.

Around 9:30, Shapiro went to Kardashian's home to inform Simpson that he needed to surrender before 11 am. That was a half hour following the time when murder charge was brought to court.

Simpson confessed to Shapiro the reason he would like to surrender himself Simpson, and police complied. They believed that a celebrity like Simpson will not try to escape. Police agreed to hold Simpson's surrender until noon, to enable him to be examined by a specialist in mental health because he had been showing indications of suicidal depression.

Simpson had revised the will of his parents and mother and had written three letters sealed for his kids: one addressed to them as well as one for his mother, and the third for the general public.

Over 1,000 journalists waited to see Simpson's perp walk in the police station. But Simpson did not show up as the schedule. The LAPD immediately informed Shapiro that Simpson would be held at the home of Kardashian.

Kardashian and Shapiro Shapiro and Kardashian told Simpson however, when police came in about an hour later Simpson as well as Al Cowlings had disappeared.

The three letters Simpson wrote was left in the mail. In the afternoon, at 1:50 pm, Command Dave Gascon, LAPD's chief spokesperson, announced that he had declared Simpson as a wanted person;

police issued an all-points notice to Simpson and an arrest warrant was issued for Cowlings.

Around 5 p.m, Kardashian and one of his lawyers for defense were reading Simpson's open note. The letter Simpson wrote a message of greetings to his 24 friends, and said "First everyone understand I had nothing to do with Nicole's murder". Simpson described his fight with Brown and the decision they made not to reconcile and pleaded with journalists "as a last wish" to not bother his kids. The letter he wrote to his girlfriend Paula Barbieri, "I'm sorry ... we're not going to have, our chance ... As I leave, you'll be in my thoughts". In addition, he wrote "I can't go on" as well as an apology for those in the Goldman family. The letter ended with "Don't feel sorry for me. I have had a great life, great friends. Please think of the real O. J. and not this lost person".

Many interpret this as suicide note. Simpson's mom collapsed when she heard the message, and journalists became involved in the search for Simpson.

In the Kardashian press conference, Shapiro claimed Simpson's psychiatrists concurred on the suicide note's interpretation. On television, Shapiro appealed to Simpson to give up.

In the early hours of 6:20 an individual from Orange County notified California Highway Patrol following the discovery of someone they thought to be Simpson driving an Bronco along the I-5 freeway that was heading to the toward the north. Police tracked the calls made by Simpson through his cellphone. In the evening, 6:45pm the police officers Ruth Dixon saw the Bronco headed north along Interstate

405 and when she saw it approaching, Cowlings yelled out that Simpson was sitting in the rear seat and pointed the gun towards his own head.

The police officer stopped and pursued the vehicle, which was speeding with a speed of 35 miles per hour (56 km/h) which included as many as 20 police vehicles accompanying her on the pursuit.

Zoey Tur of KCBS-TV was the first person to spot Simpson on the news helicopter after colleagues learned that FBI's tracking of mobile phones was able to locate Simpson in El Toro Y. El Toro Y.

Nine news helicopters were eventually part of the chase; Tur compared the fleet with Apocalypse Now, and the large number of media participants resulted in camera feeds appearing in the wrong channels. The hunt took so long that one helicopter ran out fuel and forced the station to request another helicopter for a camera feed.

Being aware that Cowlings was listening to KNX-AM radio, sportscaster Pete Arbogast called Simpson's former USC football coach John McKay and connected him with Simpson.

While both men wept, Simpson said to McKay, "OK, Coach, I won't do anything stupid. I promise" on the air. "There is no doubt in my mind that McKay stopped O.J. from killing himself in the back of that Bronco" Arbogast stated.

McKay has reiterated his radio appeal to Simpson to surrender instead of taking the suicide route: "My God, we love you, Juice. Just pull over and I'll come out and stand by you all the rest of my life".

Walter Payton, Vince Evans along with others from all over the country pleaded with Simpson via radio to surrender.

At the Parker Center, officials discussed ways to convince Simpson to surrender in peace. Lange was interviewed by Simpson concerning the murders on the 13th of June discovered that he held Simpson's mobile number and contacted him numerous times. The colleague connected an audio recorder to Lange's cell phone, and then recorded an exchange with Lange and Simpson during which Lange frequently pleaded with Simpson to "throw the gun out [of] the window" in the safety of his children and mother.

Simpson apology for his not submitting himself to police earlier in the day, and he said that Simpson wasn't "the only one who deserved to get hurt" and Simpson was "just gonna go with Nicole". Simpson demanded Lange to "just let me get to the house" and added "I need [the gun] for me". The voice of Cowlings is heard in the tape (after the Bronco arrived at the home of Simpson, which was and was surrounded by police) asking Simpson to surrender and stop the pursuit peacefully.

Los Angeles streets emptied and drinks orders were stopped in bars when people viewed the show on TV. Each television channel aired the chase. ABC, NBC, CBS, CNN, and local media outlets interrupted their regularly scheduled programs to show the chase that was seen by approximately 95 million viewers across the country. Only 90 million people had viewed the season's Super Bowl.

As NBC kept broadcasting the game 5 from the NBA Finals between the New York Knicks and the Houston Rockets at Madison Square Garden Game 5 was broadcast as a box that was small on the side and Tom Brokaw covered the chase.

The chase was broadcast live on air by ABC anchors Peter Jennings and Barbara

Walters for the five news magazines on the network and achieved the highest ratings they have ever had. In the ABC coverage, a joke message from one of the fan to Howard Stern was made to Jennings.

The chase was broadcast across the globe, and Gascon's family members from France as well as China watching him on TV.

A large number of people, including onlookers and fans lined up at the overpasses on the course of the chase. They waited for the White Bronco to arrive.

Amidst a festival atmosphere there were signs encouraging Simpson to get out of the way. Fans screaming "Go, O.J., go" The famous motto from Simpson's Hertz commercials and encouraging the behavior of a suicide-minded murder suspect enraged Jim Hill, among those making pleas for Simpson to turn himself in.

Jack Ferreira and Mike Smith were among the spectators of the pursuit, not understanding the reason; they were as if they were part of the "common emotional experience", an author wrote. they "wonder[edwhether O.J. Simpson might be able to commit suicide or escape, end up in jail or be involved in an aggressive confrontation. What ever happens this shared story brought millions of viewers stake in the story, an innate sense of being part of the story, a feeling that they were part of a drama with a national audience being developed".

Simpson claimed to have asked that he was allowed to talk to his mother prior to deciding whether or not he should give up.

The pursuit ended around 8:00 evening at the Brentwood estate which is 50 miles

(80 kilometers) farther, and Jason, his son Jason fled his home "gesturing wildly", and 27 SWAT officers were waiting.

After staying inside the Bronco for 45 minutes Simpson was released at 8.50 after he had framed his family picture and then went home for about one hour. police officials said the suspect spoke to his mother, and then drank the glass of orange juice and caused the media to smile.

Shapiro was there Shapiro arrived, Shapiro arrived, and Simpson was handed over to the authorities within a couple of minutes. Within the Bronco the police uncovered "$8,000 in cash, a change of clothing, a loaded .357 Magnum, a United States passport, family pictures, and a disguise kit with a fake goatee and mustache".

Simpson was arrested by Parker Center and taken to Men's Central Jail; Cowlings was charged with having a connection to a wanted fugitive. He was detained for bail of $250,000.

The Bronco chase, suicide note and items discovered in the Bronco weren't presented as evidence at the trial. Marcia Clark conceded that such evidence could suggest guilt but she defended her choice, citing the reaction of the public to the suicide note as evidence that the trial was tainted by Simpson's status as a celebrity.

A majority of the people which included Simpson's close acquaintance Al Michaels, interpreted his act as an admission to guilt. However, thousands of people supported him in his decision to escape the law and embraced the guilt he felt.

Simpson was looking for a quick trial. The lawyers representing the defense and prosecutor were on call throughout the months of preparation their case.

The trial started on the 24th of January in 1995, just seven months following the murders. The trial was shown on closed-circuit television camera through Court TV and in part via other cable and network news stations, over an average of 134 consecutive days. The judge Lance Ito presided over the trial at the C.S. Foltz Criminal Courts Building.

The two leading prosecutors were the Deputy District Attorneys Marcia Clark and Christopher Darden. Clark was named the primary prosecutor, as well as Darden was assigned as the co-counsel for Clark. Attorneys Hank Goldberg and William Hodgman have been successful in prosecuting prominent cases before were able to assist Clark as well as Darden.

Two prosecutor who were experts in DNA, Rockne Harmon, and George "Woody" Clarke, were summoned to testify on DNA evidence to the trial and were aided by the Prosecutor Lisa Kahn.

The prosecution claimed that violent domestic conflict within the marriage of Simpson and Brown culminated in the murder of Brown. Simpson's past of abuse Brown caused their divorce as well as his plead of to a single count for domestic abuse in the year 1989. In the evening of the murders Simpson went to a recital for his daughter. He appeared to be angry at Brown due to a black gown she was wearing that he claimed was "tight".

The former girlfriend of Simpson, Paula Barbieri, wanted to go to the recital along together with Simpson but Simpson refused to invite Paula Barbieri to the recital. She declined. Following the performance, Simpson returned home to an unanswered message from Barbieri end their friendship.

According to the trial, Simpson then drove over to the house of Brown's with the vehicle he had purchased, a Ford Bronco to reconcile their relation. As a result, after Brown was not willing to accept, Simpson killed her in an act of "final act of control".

Goldman was later seen on the scene in order to retrieve his eyeglasses, and was killed and also murdered in order to silence him, and also remove witnesses.

The prosecution later stated the prosecution claimed that Simpson went towards his Bronco before driving home after which he stopped then walked inside his house. He then took off his blood-stained clothing and put them into the bag (except his socks and glove) and put his clean clothes on and walked away towards the limousine.

In the Airport The prosecution said Simpson removed the contents of his knapsack then took off the clothing and shoes of Bruno Magli, as well as the weapon used to kill, and dumped them in the garbage before placing the knapsack into one of his luggages, and heading for his departure.

The prosecution filed an array of 108 evidences that included 61 drops blood and DNA evidence that allegedly linked Simpson with the killings.

Without witnesses The prosecution relied on DNA for the sole physical evidence connecting Simpson with the murder. The quantity of DNA evidence used in this particular case was unique, and they believed that they were able to reconstruct the crime took place with sufficient accuracy that it resembled the eyewitness accounts.

Marcia Clark stated in her opening remarks she found an "trail of blood from the Bundy Crime scene through Simpson's Ford Bronco to his bedroom at Rockingham".

Simpson's DNA has been discovered on blood samples alongside footprints of bloody feet near the victims on the Bundy crime site. The prosecution claimed that the chance of error is 1-in-9.7 billion.

* Simpson's DNA discovered in blood samples that lead away from the victims to and along the back gate of Bundy. The prosecution claimed that the likelihood of error was one-in-200.

* Simpson, Goldman, and Brown's DNA were found at the exterior of the door as well as in Simpson's Bronco. The prosecution claimed that the chance of a mistake was 1 in 21 billion.

Simpson's DNA is found in blood samples that lead from where the Bronco was kept at Simpson's Rockingham residence up to the entrance of his front door.

* Simpson, Brown and Goldman's DNA was found on the bloody glove that was found in his house.

* Simpson and Brown's DNA were discovered on a bloody pair of socks from Simpson's bedroom. The prosecution claimed that the chance of error of the DNA was 1-in-6.8 billion.

LAPD criminalist and expert in hair fiber Susan Brockbank testified on June 27, 1995. FBI Special Agent, and expert in fiber Doug Deedrick testified on June 29th, 1995. Both testified according to the following conclusions:

* The fibers in the glove that Simpson found at his house microscopically correspond to the ones discovered at the

crime scene and prove that they were one the other's partner.

* The victims and the gloves as well as two gloves, and the Blue knit cap that the killer wore were hair that was similar to Simpson. Hair in the Blue Knit cap worn by the perpetrator was embedded within the seams. This indicates that the cap was frequently worn.

* The dark blue clothing fibers were detected on the victims. The video of the Dance show which Simpson was a part of earlier in the evening has him wearing a similarly color shirt. Kato Kaelin testified Simpson continued to wear the shirt after they returned back from McDonald's however, he was not wearing it anymore after he had answered to the door of the driver of the limousine. The police scoured his house however the shirt was not located.

Hair that was similar to Goldman was discovered on Brown and clothes fibers compatible with Brown were found on Goldman. This supports the theory of prosecution that the killer murdered Brown first, followed by Goldman then returned to Brown and slice her throat. The hair that was consistent with Brown which was discovered in the Rockingham glove was ripped, which confirms the prosecutor's assertion that the killer held Brown by the hair of her head and cut her throat.

* The fibers were utilized in the 1993-1994 model period of the Ford Bronco, the same vehicle that Simpson is the owner of, were discovered on both victims' bodies, including on the knit cap as well as both gloves.

* The glove that was found at the Simpson's house belonging to the murderer included hair and fibers from

clothing that were similar to Simpson, Brown and Goldman and also fibers from the 1993-94 Ford Bronco as well as Brown's Akita dog.

On the 19th of June, FBI shoeprint specialist William J. Bodziak testified that the shoeprints with blood at the scene of the murder as well as inside Simpson's Bronco came by a rare and expensive set that was made by Bruno Magil Italian shoes. The shoes, he determined, were of size 12, which is the exact size Simpson was wearing, and were exclusively sold by Bloomingdales. There were only 29 pairs of this size were available within the U.S. and one of it was purchased from the exact same shop that Simpson usually purchases his footwear from.

Bodziak added that even though there were two footprints left at the location, only one suspect was in the scene due to the fact that they were made from the same shoe. In cross-examination, Bailey said that the perpetrator intentionally wore shoes of too big, which Bodziak rejected as "ridiculous".

Simpson has denied having the pair of "ugly ass shoes" and there was no evidence beyond circumstantial that of him having them. Bloomingdales employees Samuel Poser testified he remembered having shown Simpson these shoes however there was no record in the store that he purchased them.

While the prosecution was unable to establish the fact that Simpson was the owner of the sneakers, Bodziak testified that a identical shoeprint of blood was left in Simpson's Bronco.

Scheck claimed that Fuhrman entered the Bronco and left his footprints in the area; he also produced an image of Fuhrman standing in a pool of blood.

Bodziak acknowledged that he wasn't capable of confirming the fact that the print on the vehicle was indeed the Bruno Magli shoe, but denied the claim of Scheck as none of the footprints in the scene could be traced by Fuhrman's footwear which makes it doubtful that the shoeprint could have been made by one of the bloody prints in the Bronco.

Simpson engaged a team of prominent defense attorneys, at first led by Robert Shapiro, who was before a civil attorney who was known for his settlements his cases. He was later joined by Johnnie Cochran who was famous for her police brutality as well as civil rights issues.

The group included well-known defense lawyer F. Lee Bailey, Robert Kardashian, Harvard appeals lawyer Alan Dershowitz, his student Robert Blasier, and Dean of Santa Clara University School of Law Gerald Uelmen. Alongside Cochran, Carl E.

Douglas and Shawn Holley, Barry Schenk and Peter Neufeld were also hired as they led of the Innocence Project and specialized in DNA evidence.

Simpson's defense is said to cost anywhere between $3 million and $6 million. The media called the group with talented lawyers as"the Dream Team, while the costs for prosecution to the taxpayer were more than US$9 million.

The defense's reasonable doubt argument was characterized by the defense team as "compromised, contaminated, corrupted" in their opening arguments. They asserted that the DNA evidence proving the guilt of Simpson had been "compromised" by the mishandling by investigators Dennis Fung and Andrea Mazzola in the process of the evidence gathering process, and 100percent of the "real killer(s)" DNA disappeared from the evidence samples. The evidence was "contaminated" in the

LAPD crime lab by a criminal Collin Yamauchi, and Simpson's DNA from his reference sample was transferred to the rest of the evidences.

The other three evidences were fabricated by police and, therefore "corrupted" by police fraud. Defense lawyers also challenged the time frame, asserting that murders occurred at around 11:00 midnight the night of.

Doctor. Robert Huizenga testified on July 14, 1995, that Simpson did not have the physical strength of committing the crimes because of arthritis chronic as well as old football injuries.

The prosecution during cross-examination created an exercise film that Simpson created a couple of days before the murders. It was titled O.J. Simpson Minimum Maintenance Fitness for Men in which it was clear the fact that Simpson was not frail.

Doctor. Huizenga admitted afterwards that Simpson might have carried out the crime if he had been at "the throes of an adrenaline-rush".

Doctor. Michael Baden, a pathologist for the forensic field, said the murders took place at around 11:00 pm, which was when Simpson is believed to have an alibi. He claimed that Brown was conscious in her seat, stood, and took an oath after her throat was cut, and she claimed that Goldman was fighting his attacker for 10 minutes while lacerated in the Jugular vein.

Following the trial, Baden acknowledged that his account of Goldman's struggle for a long time wasn't true, and he admitted that his testifying against Simpson was not a good idea.

Some critics asserted that Baden deliberately gave a false statement to secure an additional $100,000 in retainer fees because, during the week prior to his testimony the doctor. Gerdes admitted that Goldman's blood was present in Simpson's Bronco even though Goldman never getting the chance in his life to have a seat involved in the Bronco.

Barry Schenk and Peter Neufeld Peter Neufeld argued that the results of DNA tests weren't trustworthy because police did not "sloppy" in collecting and keeping it away at the scene of a crime.

Fung and Mazzola admitted that they made a few mistakes in evidence collection, such as not changing gloves every time they were handling the evidence, and packaging and storing the evidence with plastic bags instead of the paper bags advised, and placing them inside the police van that was not refrigerated until up to seven hours following the collecting. They argued that this could allow bacteria to degrade each and every "real killer(s)" DNA and, consequently, make the specimens more prone to cross-contamination within the LAPD crime laboratory.

The prosecution has denied that mistakes of Fung and Mazzola altered the accuracy of the test results. They pointed out that all the evidence samples could be tested and the majority of tests were conducted in the two labs that consult with each other but not at that of the LAPD crime lab where the contamination was alleged to have occurred.

The majority of the samples that consulting labs were given were able to be tested, while Scheck and Neufeld's theories predicted that they would be unconclusive following being "100%

degraded", claims that all DNA went to bacteria's degradation wasn't true.

The prosecution has denied that contamination took place at the LAPD crime lab, too as the results would show mixed of "real killer(s)" DNA as well as Simpson's DNA, however it was found that Simpson's DNA was the only one in the lab. In addition, the prosecution noted that defense was not able to contest any of the findings by investigating the evidence itself. Marcia Clark called Scheck and Neufeld's allegations as a "smoke-screen".

The contamination claims were presented by a microbiologist, Professor. John Gerdes. He testified on the 2nd of August 1995 in court that Forensic PCR DNA match-ups are not trustworthy as well as "The LAPD crime lab has a substantial contamination problem. It is chronic in the sense that it doesn't go away". Gerdes said that, due to the history of LAPD's contamination, he wouldn't think one or all of the PCR DNA matches that were found in this instance as reliable, since the tests were performed through the LAPD. The attorney also stated the consultants' PCR DNA matches were not valid, since the test results were sent "through the LAPD" for packing and shipping. Gerdes believes that only three DNA matches as authentic, exactly the three that the defense claimed were planted by police.

When he was cross-examined during cross-examination, Dr. Gerdes admitted there was not any evidence of cross-contamination having taken place and he admitted the fact that he testified about "what might occur and not what actually did occur". The doctor acknowledged the fact that blood of victims was found in the Bronco and that Simpson's blood was in the crime scene, and that it was not due to contamination. The judge also acknowledged that there was nothing happening in the course of "packaging and shipping" that might affect those results from two laboratories that consult with each other.

The prosecution claimed the prosecution claimed that Gerdes wasn't a reliable witness, as he was not a person with previous experience with forensics, and had given testimony for criminal defendants before and has repeatedly stated that the DNA evidence they presented did not have credibility due to contamination.

Clark added that it wasn't a coincidence that the three things he first claimed were authentic were actually the same three defense witnesses claimed to have planted, while the remaining fifty-eight were false positives. He also said that the 47 controls for the substrate, which serve to identify the presence of contamination and are false positives.

Expert in DNA forensics for the defense, Dr. Henry Lee testified on August 24, 1995 and acknowledged that Gerdes's assertion proved to be "highly improbable".

Barry Schenk's lengthy cross-examination of Dennis Fung was lauded in the press. But Howard Coleman, president of GeneLex, a Seattle-based lab for forensic DNA GeneLex and GeneLex, condemned Scheck's cross-examination in the context of "smoke and mirrors" and said "Everything that we receive in our lab has been contaminated to some level. What degradation or contamination could give you unconclusive results. The result isn't"false positives".

Initial defense arguments only stated that three evidences were made by the police. However, they later claimed that all the evidence of blood against Simpson was fabricated as part of the course of a conspiracy by police.

The prison nurse was accused by the police Thano Peratis, criminalists Dennis Fung, Andrea Mazzola, and Colin Yamauchi, and Vannatter and Fuhrman and Fuhrman of being part of an attempt to catch Simpson.

In his closing argument, Cochran called Fuhrman and Vannatter "twins of deception" and advised the jury that they should remember Vannatter for "the man who carried the blood" as well as Fuhrman in the role of "the man who found the glove".

In the closing argument Darden dismissed the idea that officers from the police force might be tempted to indict Simpson. Darden asked why even if LAPD were in opposition to Simpson in the first place, they would have gone to the house eight times in response to assault calls made in the case of Brown in the years 1986 to 1988, but they did not take him into custody; They only indicted him for abuse charges on January 29, 1989. photographs of Brown's face were incorporated into the records.

Darden pointed out that the police were not able to take any action against Simpson for five days following the killings in 1994. In the closing arguments of the prosecution, Cochran and Scheck very prominently objected 771 times, in an effort to reduce the impact of their arguments on juries even although Ito did not overrule sixty-nine times but he didn't once to admonish Cochran as well as Scheck or threat them with disobedience to court due to their actions.

In his summary before the jury the jury, he could not challenge any of the prosecution's allegations, so he concentrated his argument entirely on criticizing the LAPD specifically Fuhrman, Lange, and Vannatter. Cochran emphasized Fuhrman was found to be repeatedly used to refer to blacks as the"n-word" and boasted about beating young black males while working as police officers.

Cochran also compared Fuhrman with Adolph Hitler, and described him as "a genocidal racist, a perjurer, America's worst nightmare and the personification of evil" as well as claimed with no any evidence to show that Fuhrman put the glove in place to try and frame Simpson as the perpetrator of the crime solely because of his dislike of couples who were interracial.

Cochran provided a separate piece of paper that bore the name "Vannatter's Big Lies", and claimed, without evidence or proof that Vannatter was back at the scene of crime using Simpson's blood and deposited the blood there, even though Vannatter being previously a witness that he'd given the blood an heir to Dennis Fung in order to keep the evidence from becoming misplaced.

Cochran described Fuhrman vannatter and Fuhrman as "two devils of deception" He also urged jurors "stop this cover-up" and "acquit Simpson and send the police a message", that was taken by some as an unintentional appeal for juror nullification.

In the wake of his report After his summary, Cochran faced many death threats and appointed bodyguards from Louis Farrakhan.

Responding, Fred Goldman, who was also Jewish was quoted by Cochran himself, describing him as "the worst kind of racist ever" and called him a "sick man" for comparing Fuhrman with Hitler and comparing himself to Farrakhan who was thought of as a racist and anti-Semite. Robert Shapiro, also Jewish said that the incident was particularly offensive to him. Cochran making comparisons between Fuhrman's assertions and the Holocaust in claiming that any comparison was not even remotely possible.

In an interview with Vincent Bugliosi's assessment of the matter, Vannatter said that he was mad by Cochran's accusations against him, he was possessed by the urge to slap his opponent in the courtroom.

The fear grew that riots of race like the ones that occurred that occurred in 1992, might take place all over Los Angeles and the rest of the nation in the event that Simpson was found guilty of murder. The result was that the majority of Los Angeles police officers were assigned 12-hour shifts.

The police had arranged for over 100 officers riding on horses to guard the Los Angeles County courthouse on the day that the verdict was made public to prevent riots in the large crowd. The president Bill Clinton was briefed on the security precautions if there were riots expected to be widespread.

The sole testimony jurors considered was the limo driver's testimony. Park.

On Wednesday, October 3 1995 Simpson got acquitted of each count of murder. The jury reached its verdict at around 3:00 pm on the 2nd of October, after a four-hour discussion, however it delayed the release until. Following the reading of the verdict by juror nine, 44 year old Lionel Cryer, gave Simpson the black power hand salute.

The New York Times reported that Cryer was an ex-member of the nationalist revolutionary Black Panther Party that prosecutors had "inexplicably left on the panel".

The estimated number of people around the world watched or heard the decision's announcement. Call volume for long distances dropped by 58% and the volume of trading at the New York Stock Exchange decreased by 41 percent. The use of water decreased because people were avoiding bathrooms. There was so much to be done because of the decision that it resulted in an estimated cost of 480 million dollars in reduced work.

The U.S. Supreme Court received an announcement on the decision in oral arguments. the justices passing the message to one another as they listened to the attorney's argument.

Congressmen cancelled press conferences including Joe Lieberman telling reporters,

"Not only would you not be here, but I wouldn't be here, either".

In the month of November, Regan Books announced a book written by Pablo Fenjves that was based on the interviews of Simpson called If I Did it, a story that publishers claimed was an imagined confession. The publication was scheduled to coincide with the airing of a Fox show that starred Simpson.

On the 20th of November News Corporation canceled the project in response to criticism from the public.

Then in the future, the Goldman family received rights to the novel and it was published under the name"If I Did It: Confessions of the Killer.

Chapter 5: Amelia Earhart

The moment Amelia Earhart walked into the room, Cimarron could not typically come to a quick conclusion about her being the famed missing aviator...except due to the fact that the man had been battling with ghosts that had appeared for a long time and her Aviator glasses and the long coat she was wearing caused him to believe it was Amelia Earhart.

Amelia sent her account from her newspaper to Cimarron for the following information:

Amelia Earhart disappeared along with her navigator Fred Noonan, on July 2nd, 1937. They were spotted over Central Pacific Ocean near Howland Island.

They last saw each other at Lae, New Guinea, on the 2nd of July 1937. It was their final stop on land before Howland Island and one of their last legs of the journey. There is a general consensus that Noonan and Noonan were killed somewhere in the Pacific on the way to their final destination, only three weeks before her birthday.

A little over a year and six months later, after Noonan as well as Noonan went missing, Earhart was officially declared to be dead.

Public interest and investigations about their disappearances persist over 80 years after their disappearance.

Earhart was well-known before her disappearance in 1932 for her Transatlantic Solo flight.

The flight lasted 14 hours and 56 mins in which she had to contend against strong winds from the north, frozen conditions, and mechanical issues, Earhart landed in a pasture in Culmore located in the north of Derry, Northern Ireland. The landing was watched by Cecil King and T. Sawyer. A farm worker was asked "Have you flown far?" Earhart said, "From America"

The year 1935 was the time that Earhart became a part of Purdue University as a guest faculty member for women to help them find career options and also as an advisor for the Department of Aeronautics.

The year was 1936 when Earhart set out to plan a world-wide flight. Though others had also sailed across the globe, her journey would be the longest, with 29,000 miles (47,000 kilometers) since it took a mostly equatorial path, and using funding from Purdue.

In her second try at an around the globe flight the last voice message received at Howland Island from Earhart indicated that she and Noonan were traveling along the line of a position (running N-S, 157-

337°) that Noonan could have calculated as well drawn in a map to indicate that they were passing through Howland.

When all communication was cut off to Howland Island, attempts were attempted to contact those flyers via vocal and Morse Code transmissions. Operators from the Pacific as well as the United States may have heard messages from the sunk Electra however, they were either unintelligible or shaky.

A few of these reported transmissions were later found to be hoaxes while other were considered to be authentic.

A study of the bearings at Pan American Airways stations suggested signals that originated from several places such as Gardner Island (Nikumaroro), 360 miles (580 kilometers) towards the SSE.

At the time, it was emphasized in the moment that if these signals originated emanating from Earhart as well as Noonan then they must be on the ground together with the plane since the water could have sucked out the Electra's electric system.

There were sporadic signals reported about four to five days after disappearance but they never gave any concrete data. Captain of the USS Colorado later said: "There was no doubt many stations were calling the Earhart plane on the plane's frequency, some by voice and others by signals. All of these added to the confusion and doubtfulness of the authenticity of the reports."

In the hour following the last message recorded by Earhart The USCGC Itasca undertook an ultimately unsuccessful search to the west and north in Howland Island based on initial beliefs about the transmissions coming by the aircraft.

The United States Navy (USN) quickly joined in the search, and in around three days, they sent equipment to the search zone in the vicinity of Howland Island.

The first search conducted of the Itasca included running along the 157/337 position line towards the NNW starting from Howland Island. The Itasca was then able to search for the region to the northeast of the island. in the same area however, it was larger than the region that was searched towards the NW.

Based on the bearings from several alleged Earhart radio communications however, some search efforts focused on an exact location on the 281 degree line (approximately north) away from Howland Island without evidence of the flying birds.

A few days following Earhart's first authentic radio signal on the 6th of July 1937 the captain of the battleship

Colorado was issued an order by the commandant of the Fourteenth Naval District to take charge of all coastal and naval guards units in order to coordinate the search effort.

Amelia took a seat beside Cimarron and exclaimed, "The girls told me that you are 'The Messenger' who is going to get the truth out to the world and solve all of its mysteries."

"And who may I ask are the girls?"

"Why, Nicole, Marilyn and Natalie, of course."

"Geez, I don't know what to make of any of this, but what is your message, Ameila?"

"Well, I thought that there were some folks who might like to know what really happened to me, the day I disappeared."

"OK, Amelia, I'd love to share your experience to all of the people of the world. What was the event that occurred on the day you vanished?"

"Well there are many who believe the story that Fred and I were unable to fuel on that day, crashed, and sank...but some believe we were able to land on an island, but weren't discovered.

We are 200 miles away away from Howland Island.

Itasca, the USS Coast Guard cutter Itasca was planned to be the radio link to our communication contact.

When the plane departed from the island, they expected to be in radio communication with Itasca. In the event of radio contact it should be able to utilize the radio directions (RDF) to direct the plane towards Itasca as well as Howland.

The plane wasn't receiving an radio signal from Itasca therefore it couldn't determine the specific RDF bearing. While Itasca received HF radio signals from the aircraft, it was not equipped with an HF RDF equipment. As such, it was unable to determine whether it was bearing on the plane.

Nearly no messages were sent on the plane.

Thus that the plane wasn't guided to Howland but was instead completely on its own, and with a limited amount of fuel. The plane landed on the sun's parallel line, and began searching for Howland in that location.

I transmitted: "We must be on you but cannot see you - but gas is running low. Have been unable to reach you by radio. We are flying at 1,000 feet."

In the morning, at 8:43 am At 8:43 am, I informed the police, "We are on the line 157 337. We will repeat this message. We will repeat this on 6210 kilocycles. Wait."

Between my low-on-fuel signal at 7:42 AM and my last message that was confirmed at 8:43 am, our signal strength continued to be consistent, suggesting that we did not leave the immediate Howland zone when we were running empty of gas.

The U.S. Coast Guard made this decision by observing the strength of our signal in the vicinity of the island and observing that our signal strength was based on reports from 100 and 200 miles away. These reports occurred about 30 minutes apart and provide important information on the ground speed.

Based on the above facts in addition to the fact that I did not receive any further signal from me, Coast Guard first responders initiating the search determined that they had run out of fuel near and to the to the north Howland.

"To be brutally honest, and you know I love you Fred," Amelia turned toward the navigator Fred Noonan "Fred miscalculated the fuel needed to get to Howland Island."

Fred gave a smug smile as he hunched his shoulders and raised his hands toward the sky, like he was saying "mistakes happen."

Amelia added "Navy aircrafts of the USS Colorado carried out a meticulous survey of Gardner Island, but I could have informed them they'd find no evidence. In the meantime, I as well as Fred had moved in together with Davey Jones.

Some other brilliant minds believed that we were taken captive in the hands of Japanese. This is a great idea it is that one.

One possibility was that said we crash-landed on the island Saipan in the distance of 2700 miles away far from Howland Island. A conversation with an Saipanese female, the woman said that Fred and I were killed at the hands of Japanese soldiers. Rubbish!"

"There was a few who believed I conducted spy missions on behalf of FDR. Other people claimed I played the character as Tokyo Rose but authentic voice tests disproved that absurdity.

The most memorable is the one that said I escaped the terror and relocated into New Jersey, remarried, and was renamed Irene Craigmile Bolam.

Bolam claimed to be me and filed a lawsuit against McGraw-Hill to get a book that claimed that I am Irene Bolam, which was later proved to be a lie account. I am not Irene Bolam.

Chapter 6: Little Boy Ghost

Date posted the date was June 28, 1998.

My dad and mom purchased the house in 1973, just a time before my birth. It was a fixer-upper not to mention and a 250-year-old Cape style house on the back roads of Maine. A family lived in the house for decades until the day it was sold off. There is a rumor that the house was once used for the purpose of running slaves in the past as well as that a person who was connected to the family that resided in the house shot himself in the field behind and the land close to the house is burial site of an earlier local group of Native Americans. This is a historic house that bears the marks of various inhabitants as well as renovations.

My parents worked to bring the home so that they could reside in it. They needed to replace their fire places (there are three fireplaces, each one on a central flue) as well as build steps into the basement, as the cellar was just an opening in the floor as well as the ladder. Then they had to complete various other things with doors and windows.

My mom tells me that often, when she worked alone within the house, objects were found being missing. In particular, she recalled making use of a screwdriver to remove the dirt out of between the flooring boards. Then she put it away for a quick trip to get drinks, but when she returned, the dirt had disappeared. My mom believes in the paranormal. So she placed her hands on her hips, and declared, "Now, I'm trying to fix this house up, and if you keep hiding things on me it isn't going to help." She then left the room for a couple of minutes, then was relaxed. When she came back, the screwdriver, it was right in the spot where it had been left.

My father, who is the most skeptical person and doesn't believe in any type of supernatural phenomena is working in the cellar that afternoon. He had warned my brother, who was only three at that time, to not enter the hole in the cellar since there was no staircase in place and he could get swept in. My father was climbing up the ladder that was in the basement and his head had reached the same height of the floor, when he noticed the feet of a child wearing shorts and sneakers running past the hole. The thought was that the child was my brother my dad shouted, "Billy! I thought I told you to stay away from this hole!" My mother heard it and rushed inside to ask the man what was wrong. After my dad explained to her about what he observed she explained she thought Billy was out with her playing in the backyard.

My dad was able to see this child twice. The other night, he lay down on the sofa as he watched television. He was awakened by that spooky late-night static. Then he looked around and was greeted by a fair-haired young child in his striped pajamas on the couch, cross-legged, in front of the television. In his mind, he thought it might be my younger brother, who was fair-haired and young also, he offered, "Billy, go to bed." The child resisted and repeated the request. The child then looked at my father, but the child wasn't even my brother. The child then went away.

My mom also saw the little boy. In the night, she awoke to see the child dressed in his striped pajamas sitting in front of the windows next to her bed watching at the outside. The girl thought that it was Billy (poor kid was blamed for every thing) and told him, "Billy, go to bed." She was ignored by the child when she repeated the request and then, you're guessing it -- the kid was not Billy. She describes it as disappearing in a way that it seemed to collapse into itself. It was like "water going down a drain" the way she described it after which it vanished. My dad woke up and was quite shaken over the entire incident.

This is all for tonight and I'll be back with to write about in the future. An interesting note to close with... My brother spent a day running around our chickens' pen, as well as harassing the animals (I did not mention that I was raised in an agricultural farm). The nightmare he had was in the evening that a gigantic chicken was perched in the bed's footboard bed and was pecking at his head. He says the chicken was alive and the chicken that was huge actually existed. The noise woke my mom. She ran off to the room of her son, but the chicken vanished.

What moral lessons can I apply in my tales? Do not run around the home, we came up with this idea before Poltergeist the film. Also, show compassion to animals. Goodnight!

Children Calling

Date of receipt: February 2, 2002.

Hey All!

It's my first time writing a post on this website or on any other site to be honest, but I hope that you enjoy the things I've got to say.

I've always had an interest in the supernatural, even though I have been a fervent Christian I've experienced a few experiences up until the time I reached the 8th year of school. This is my very first major encounter. I'm not certain what caused it, or even the source of it However, it terrified the crap out of me.

It was around 11:00 at night on a school day when I was in my bedroom when my mom called me and asked me to and let my dogs inside. I raced through the steps toward the back of the door, then opened it. My dogs were immediately greeted with the names. Bo, the younger dog Bo was flying across into the "bridge." It was a part of my deck at the back that linked the backyard to the deck and led to a massive ditch, which was dug to make sure it could be accessed from beneath my swimming pool. Bo was flying past me and into my house. Another animal, Alex, who was significantly older than me, at 13, at that time could not join in.

It was extremely cold and it was windy at night but the wind wasn't creating any noise. If you were standing at the entrance and looked out into the backyard, directly to your left was a massive oak tree. I was beginning to experience an unsettling feeling when I listened to what was like the sound of children's voices coming out of the trees. They were yelling something which sounded similar to my name.

Then I began to panic and shouted Alex's name. Alex finally made it to the bridge, but stopped just near the point at the point where the stairs are. Because he was old, there was arthritis in the hips. He was also unable to walk up the steps without help. Then, I could hear the people calling. The voices grew more loud and quickly became apparent that there were two children asking my name. I started to scream in terror and anxiety. The fear of these voices and the fear that they might cause harm to my pet. But there was absolutely nothing I could do to get in the direction of pursuing him.

The noises grew more intense and they giggled when they talked. I replied with a firm "no" under my breath and shut the door, not inviting the dog inside. I ran up the steps to the bedroom of my parents and loudly stated, "That stupid dog won't come in. You get him." After that, I sat into my bedroom, closed my blinds, settled into bed and attempted to go to sleep.

It is clear that the voices were not "live" children because at the time that it occurred, it was late at night and it was a night at school, and they sounded young. The houses around mine were not home to children, or if they did what could they do in my front yard around eleven at night on a school day? The kids couldn't cross my fence, anyway.

The incident was only the start of my experience. When I later told the story again to my mom and she was a bit agitated, however she believed in me. If you'd like you can read other stories to share and will forward them to you to you if you'd want to.

Bubble People

The date of publication is October 15, 1995.

Hey here. I've been following you for a while. length of time and have posted occasionally with a question or comment. However, many of the posts have brought back some memories from the home in which I was raised. I decided it would be enjoyable to tell these stories and try to return to the community that has been a source of inspiration for me to reflect on. The text may be lengthy therefore you can decide to print it and then read it at time.

The first step is to let me talk a little about the building in general. It is located on "The Avenues" of Salt Lake City, Utah and was constructed in the early 1800s. For added ambiance it has one of the biggest cemetery in the country just on the other side of it. I had a lot of fun being a kid who lived just a few blocks from graveyards, especially during Halloween. But I'm not sure if it did anything with strange happenings that occurred within the home.

The usual noises of an old home--the creaks and groans, and occasionally steps on the steps. The basement was creepy, just like the majority of basements. One room was within the basement it was particularly troubling. There was no one who ever entered there, unless absolutely needed. There was no reason for anyone to stay the room for longer than they needed to. My younger brother and I could think we were watching eyes over us from the dark space at times.

Our family moved into the home in the year my brother was around three or four and my birth to the family shortly following. My "experiences" tended to center around my brother. It was easy to empathize with dealing with an unruly younger sister who was constantly playing with toys, and constantly chasing after his every move.

My brother's dreams were numerous that made it appear as if the house was attempting to speak with the house. I was told of numerous dream experiences where the home "told" him about previous residents. One of them was that of children writing in the walls of the living area with an adult possibly a parent, shouting at the kids. A few days later they decided to make some changes in the room, and held the "wall stripping" party. Families and friends stayed at home at the house, scraping away what appeared to be thousands of different layers of wallpaper and paint. It was evident that one layer had written writing that looked like marker and crayons of words such as "1 + 1 = 2." My brother and me told my parents about this dreams the man had experienced, but they dismissed it as just a little flimsy imagination. My father passed away a few years ago. in death, while my mother remains a staunch believer of the supernatural.

The upstairs was comprised of the hallway that had my brother's room at the one side, and my own room to the left. My brother and me were living in distinct bedrooms. My brother had seven or eight posters hung on the walls of his bedroom in the moment, with ones on the ceiling as well as hanging on the walls. I was on my bed, reading, at the time when I heard the posters fall. In awe of what had transpired when I went to the room of my brother and saw the man sitting on his bed, looking of amazement. Each poster fell simultaneously! At this point, we were used to odd events and accepted them as an innocent ghost playing around.

A different incident occurred when I was between nine and 10 years old. My friend and I were having fun playing "school" in a room that was turned to be an study. I was on the ground, drawing on a chalkboard while my companion was making up homework from the book. My parents were working on any kind of work within the home. the space was used for storage of junk. Therefore, it wasn't unusual to see a piece of wood laying across the floor, right near my leg. This particular piece featured a sharp end it began to poke my legs. I was trying to focus at my work on the chalkboard, and did not pay thought to it until I noticed. I assumed that my friend was accidentally moving it around. This became annoying which is why I decided to instruct my friend not to poke me with this piece wood. I then noticed she was straying across the room but not near me, or even the wood!

Similar incidents would occur and it was just a couple of small warnings that another person besides us was in the home. Parents didn't seem to be a bit bothered by any of it however, and they always assured us that this was simply our imagination.

They weren't often considered to be a joke, but. I did recall having the experience of seeing "the bubble people" at late at night. They looked like tiny, round, vibrant lighting fixtures that floated over my living room. They were typically visible from the corner my eyes. Their faces displayed smiles of joy, glee and joy. They scared me at first and then would rush downstairs to my mother she would then take me to my bed, and then tell that it was all my imagination.

A few nights ago, I lay in bed and trying to get some sleep, as I spotted a huge "bubble person" by my bedroom's door. It was an extremely dim night and he appeared in a vivid way, just hanging in the air. Also, in contrast to most of the bubble people that I witnessed, he wasn't gone as I looked at him. He wasn't quite like the others. He actually had an almost sly appearance to his face. He was also multi-colored, rather than a single solid color this was also unusual in the world of bubbles.

After looking at each other for some time and then I decided to take close to glance. In a bid to regain all the courage I had and determination, I climbed from bed and toward it, never letting my eyes off of its glistening face. It was then that I realized I think this was my brother and his cousin (who was living in our home at the time) trying to make me feel scared! It actually was a bit like the mask that my brother had made at the school. As I breathed a sigh satisfaction, I hit the mask, to let the fools I was able to catch their humorous quip. I was astonished when my hand swung right through the mask, but it was there just in front of me. Incredulous, I ran downstairs to my mom weeping and crying. She told me it was all my imagination. She continued to hold me until I was asleep.

A few years later, I discovered that my brother had also seen the bubble people and finally we decided this might not have been an imagination after all.

There was a cream-colored soft-padded sectional sofa in our living room. It, like to velvet, appeared to lighten or darken as you stroked the material one way or in the opposite direction. My brother and me were watching the TV and I spotted an exact skull engraved on the sofa's back. I was thinking that maybe my brother may have "drawn" it there with his fingers in the past, but I informed him that it was attractive. The couch was a blank space. and admitted that he had not drawn the thing. He then pointed out other parts of the skeleton: the leg, torso and the arms. Everything was perfectly proportional, as if an artist had created the skeleton. My parents were absent during this period and nobody was in the home. Who could possibly have drawn this creepy skeleton in the couch? It scared me to death which is why I was able to brush away the creature, never to be able to find it back in the future.

My aunt traveled all over across the globe and left wonderful souvenirs to us. One present she bought me was a doll made of crochet which I believe was Brazil. It seemed spooky for me but I didn't really like it. However, it came from an affectionate relative, and was my own.

There were many times I'd see the doll in the room of my brother. I was always angry by him taking my doll and return it to place where it belongs, it was located on the lower bookcases because I was unable to rest in it's bedroom. Naturally, it found it's way back to the room of my brother. As I would shout at him to take my doll away then he'd say that he believed I placed it in the room. He wasn't a fan of this doll as much.

We then moved out of our home to a condominium located on the Upper East Side. I didn't remember packing the doll. Neither my mom or brother. Actually it was as if we all appeared to have forgotten about the doll. However, a couple of days later after we moved into our new house, the doll was in my brother's bedroom.

As my brother retreated He left the doll at the top of my bookshelf, that I would keep it. It was then that one day the doll was no longer on the shelves. Then, as it turned out, when we visited my brother at his new home There was the doll. I brought the doll up to my brother and told him that he ought to be able to tell me that the doll was his. However, he said I didn't ask him to take it. After a few years after that, he relocated from the apartment to a different one, leaving the doll at his old home for new tenants. He was unhappy with the doll and did not want to keep it. The doll accompanied him into his new house and was found inside one of the boxes. He eventually accepted the fact the fact that he'd never in a position to eliminate it, and he simply packed it away each time it was time to move.

Chapter 7: Closet Monster

Date of reception: September, 1998

At the age of 12 years old, my dad gave me a Ouija board. It was the standard type that is sold in toy stores. I wasn't aware of the use of the board until a few years afterwards, so naturally I did not follow the guidelines. I played with it on my own I didn't let it go in the middle as I left the hand piece pointing towards the floor when I removed it. I stored this board inside the closet that was within our computer room. It was located right beside the computer.

A few days ago I was at home by myself playing on our laptop, which was next to our closet. The door leading to the closet was shut, which is a good thing. When I was working on the computer, I heard something growl inside the closet. Then something started to bang against the door, as if it were trying to open it. It was clear that the door banging. It was any kind of earthquake, and I'm sure we don't hear earthquakes like that. There was only me at home and the dog was out. I did not bother looking inside the closet because I was racing out of the room at the speed I could. I ran outside, and then down the street, waiting until my mom returned to get home.

I was not aware of the incident until I turned at the age of 18. I didn't even use the board again until I was 18. At the time, I had watched the film Witchboard and believed that I'd done some wrong. There was a person I knew in that moment who knew pretty much everything about supernatural phenomena. I explained to him the subject and he threw the board and threw it away. I'm not sure what the guy used it for.

Some time ago, in my 20s, I spoke to my younger sister. There were four of us and

I'm the oldest and she's 10 years older than me. In some way, the computer room came up. I told her that I was scared to go into the room because it felt terrifying. Her eyes grew large and she began to tell me how she was afraid about it, too. It was like it was a place where something had gone missing. I reminisced with her about an experience from years ago. It was a relief to know somebody else was also scared of that space and was not just a figment of my imagination.

There's a little less than a percentage chance that my parents' home being haunted. The house was constructed in the 70s, and just one family lived there. I have known the family, as well. No one has ever died within the area. Before the houses were constructed on the land, the whole area was used as a farmland. There can't be spirits that came from there. What I could think of is that something was a part of the plan. I'm wondering if it's in the room. My sister and me still are in a relationship with that room.

China Cabinet Date in March of 1999.

It's an all-new house that is just two years old situated in a subdivision that is brand new.

The most bizarre incident that occurred was one year ago or so. This home has an open layout. This means the dining area, living room, and kitchen all form the same space. Bedroom 1 is situated on one side of the home while the two other bedrooms are situated on the other. In order to go from the master bedroom to another room, take a straight path through the living space.

In the end, I was tidying up my the house and went through a few magazines, and placed them down in an organized heap next to the garbage bin. I continued to clean around the entire house. After about 10 hours in my master bedroom I took a break to walk across the property. In my path was the most popular magazine I'd placed on the floor of the kitchen. The magazine had somehow moved its way across the space.

Then, when I got home after work, I walked into the master bathroom and "something" had removed about five combs and brushes, and put them perfectly across the bathroom vanity.

The other time, I was working in the kitchen, cleaning dishes, wiping the counters or the counter. I turned my back to the sink, then turned to see the sponge as well as the holder of its metal sitting right in the middle of an aluminum sink. If it fell on the floor, it might not be as perfect and could cause the metal to metal clack. There's been a myriad of other objects that have been which were mysteriously removed from this area.

There has been footsteps in the dining room. They've been bold also. In the six months since we've moved here, there have been knocks on the walls and doors open on their own. My bedroom door hit the floor in the middle of the night as we tried to sleep. Also, twice I've heard the voice of a man close to me, saying "Pssst!" Many times, I've asked my husband "What did you say?" When I heard a male's voice and he claims there was nothing said.

We also have a cabinet for china that will not stay shut. The cabinet is open before our eyes. At the moment, I've got it secured with twist-ties. It's got a story. My grandmother owned a rental unit as well as a group of renters that my mother would describe my mother as "some strange cult" left a collection of furniture inside the unit. Cabinet was among the furniture pieces. There are a number of rappers rapping on the wall to the wall it is on.

We're sorry for taking so long. This could be an edited version of the original, but.

Mine Road

Date of receipt: October, 1997

The story didn't actually occur in a coal mine however, it has a connection to the mining industry.

22 Mine Road. There is a legend about the road, that you can be driven up in the event that you slow down. It's a lie, however this is only one of many urban legends that have been circulating on the basis about the mining road. It is like this. This is the way in which the story was relayed to me by my grandfather.

22 Mine Road is located between Williamson, West Virginia and Logan, West

Virginia. In the 20th century, coal mining was done by hand. Mining workers would make holes into the walls of mines and then fill them with dynamite. Then they would dump the rubble onto carts.

A day later, John (made up, naturally) had arrived late to his shift. So he hugged his wife before running to the exit. While sitting at the kitchen table the wife Mary was shocked to see that he'd put his lunch down there. Mary decided to bring the food to John.

Mary put on her finest coat before leaving her house with a determination to capture John prior to he hid underground. The woman walked for several minutes but was unable to locate John. She was near the end of the 22 Mine Road.

Convinced that John had just started his work, Mary stalked up the hill hoping to meet anyone who could offer her beloved husband lunch. Mary never did make it.

The mountain was shaken by a rumbling pathway. Mary recognized that it was a blast from dynamite and wasn't worried. Her experience with them was good. In front of her, she spotted an eerie cloud of dust. She was also not concerned.

Two mules loaded with carts were speeding through the mountains. Mary was right in their way and couldn't move out of their way.

Then, when John and other miners left the mine, in search of the mules terrified by the blast they discovered Mary's jacket ripped and bloody on the side on the roadway. There was no sign of Mary.

This concludes the story of the 22 Mine Road. The following is the tale as it was relayed to me in the morning by my grandpa. I'm unable to confirm the authenticity of the story however I doubt Grampa will make up the story.

My grandfather drove an old coal truck for money. He didn't have a place to put it in his the house, so he'd keep it in a locked garage on the Mine Road and drive his vehicle to his home.

A few nights ago, he tried something like this. He was driving down the road, when his truck was destroyed. It was close to the bottom of the 22 Mine Road, so he chose to return and attempt parking his coal truck. The only issue was that he didn't have no flashlight.

He began to drive and saw a light shining on the trees that were in mid-distance. The light was green, and moved toward the road. Grampa believed that it was a vehicle, therefore he did not think to think twice before walking toward it. Then, he realized that he had been mistaken.

The bright light that Grampa discovered, came from a ball that floated just a couple of feet above the surface. Unafraid of nothing in the world, and enthralled by the nature of this phenomenon, Grampa took a step toward it. The sphere moved to the back. Grampa took a step forward. The light in the room was moving in the opposite direction.

Grampa was running towards the sphere but it maintained the distance between the two. The bright light seemed to shine on the pathway. The light lasted for a while before Grampa was looking at his coal-powered truck. The light went out, and Grampa was never to experience something similar to this.

Is this the spirit that was "Mary," leading my Grandfather back to safety? Perhaps it was an angel or guardian spirit? The man doesn't have any idea. (Actually He doesn't even think about it, but if he is unable to feel it, he can't think it's true.)

I hope you enjoyed this. I'm looking for someone to tell me more details about Mary. Mary's ghost is believed to travel the streets I believe. If I come across a tale concerning her, I'll publish this too, if anyone's curious.

Chapter 8: Church Ghost

Date of posting Nov. 1997

I'm republishing this article to all those who are following the latest stories from the church that I used to be a part of, including the infamous YMCA that was added building attached to the church. The church continues as haunted by the people working in the church. This is an account that I posted several months ago.

In my teens and extremely active at my local church, I took the one in charge of decorating our basement of the church for a Halloween event we planned the night before. That was to the time when people did not feel the need to have a P.C. The church was not in problems with having hosting a Halloween celebration. I received the keys to the church because nobody was expected to allow us in on that particular day. My partner and I allowed ourselves inside and carefully secured the door behind us.

Then we went into the basement to set up our decorations. The atmosphere was peaceful and there was no music on. Then, we noticed that there were footsteps from the sky. The footsteps echoed around and around the church located directly above. We walked to the telephone and, thank God is right in front of us and asked the police to help. We didn't go up the stairs or attempt to get to know who or what that was involved because, honestly we were frightened.

Then, very quickly, a kind policeman arrived. As we allowed him into the church and he was able to see from our expressions that we were extremely angry. The officer conducted an extensive inspection of the church beginning with the second floor before going down into the basement. He also opened the back doors to the church, and swung a flag at people who were rushing by the garbage truck to ask whether they'd seen any in the area. They didn't.

The man assured us that everything was fine and then we headed back downstairs in order to get our names, along with some other details for his report which he'd later prepare.

Incredibly, while we talked, footsteps returned right above our heads. It was clear that my eyes were larger than saucers, as they matched the policeman's large eyes. My friend's teeth began to chatter because she was scared. Then there was an instant of silence, and then he said with a calm tone, "I don't know about you, but I'm getting out of here."

We were out of the building before you even had a chance to blink. My coat was even left in the car to pick later. I often think that, looking back several years after, that we resembled the scene of a Marx Brothers moment, all of us attempting to get out of the house all at once. It is often interesting to think about what he said about his findings.

A few years later, my dad who was the Scoutmaster at that church, who had his sessions in the sub-basement and told me that it was common to hear mysterious noises from the basement. The same father had also heard footsteps.

We are certain that a man died within the church. Actually, he passed away within my father's arms. A gent of a certain age, he suffered a heart attack when he arrived for church. And while he was falling, my father swarmed his body. The man wasn't an active member of our church and had never met him prior to. However, we are unable to be sure if the death of his friend occurred either before or shortly after hearing the footsteps.

The church also was home to the "annex" which seemed equally infected, yet was much more terrifying, as no one could be allowed to enter it without a companion. The church's footsteps were terrifying for us because we were aware that they weren't welcome there However, they didn't bring the sense of terror commonly felt within"the "annex" part of the church. The annex was a former YMCA and I'm certain there were diverse stories to share. It was odd that the sole "ghost" that I actually encountered was a woman. I'd love to learn what the tale behind this elusive spirit.

Cookie Ghost

Date of reception: January 1998

Hi, all. I wrote this post around two years ago on A.F.G.S., and I can't find the original article. But I'll try to keep writing as much as I'm able to remember, because I thought it was quite funny.

A few of my buddies and I gathered to have a storytelling gathering. Anything was permissible, however because the one person, Josh, freaked everyone out by his encounter with the spirit of a guardian in the state park and we chose to create a ghoulish sort of night. The stories were all kind of frightening, and one of my acquaintances who is always optimistic, was thinking she could lighten up the mood. This is, in a sense, the story Kitty shared with me.

Kitty knew a person who lived in a big style, plantation Southern home. A cottage was situated across the street of the home her parents would rent out. The first time they let it out to a couple comprising one husband and wife and a small child.

In this moment, the focus changes towards the wife of the newly arrived residents. Her husband, along with her daughter often left at weekends and head out to the town to shop as well as other chores. After living at the cottage for couple of weeks, they returned home one Sunday to find freshly baked cookies baking in the oven. The wife was thinking, "Am I going crazy? Nobody got any ingredients out to make cookies. Did they?" Then she sought out her husband, as well as their family on the hill. Both responded in a negative manner.

It was a constant occurrence over and over again, forcing them to believe the ghost was an entity of some kind as they couldn't see anyone else in the act to play a joke with them. The manifestations did not become evident, however they were able to have fresh baked cookies every time they took a trip out for the afternoon. In the end the couple decided to relocate as they were worried about the possibility of other manifestations that would be a threat to their daughter. They decided to leave, and two gentlemen took over the house.

Then when we are back, the camera goes to the parents of Kitty's best friend whom they had not informed them about the ghost inside the cottage. They observed that the men continued to stay for one year and they wondered if ghosts had been revealing itself. The mother of the family of"the "big house" went down to inquire about the state of affairs. In the absence of any response the mother asked "You haven't, um, had any unusual experiences happen in the past year, have you?"

One of them stared at her and told her, "Oh, you mean the ghost? Oh, we love him. He makes cookies for us at least once a week."

Happy haunting!

Convenience Store Ghost

The date of posting was May 25, 1995.

Hey, it's been quite awhile since I've wrote, but here's an authentic ghostly story that comes of the checkered streets of convenience stores that run through Tucson, AZ, The Circle K Phantom, as it was recounted to me by Gwen.

My best friend Gwen was a clerk job at different convenience stores throughout town in order to help her get through her college. The time of leaping between 7-Eleven, Quick Mart to Circle Ks was roughly between 1990 and 1992. Her first gig was the tiny Circle K in a somewhat peaceful neighborhood located on the south end of town. The shift ran from

10:10 until 6:00 AM. Yes, that's right--the graveyard shift.

The first few days were bustling. An engineering team built an off ramp for one of the freeways that runs through town in the evening and Gwen was able to enjoy a booming sales from the loud and muscular people. Work was finished in about a month, and the business was slowed down dramatically.

To pass the clock, Gwen brought in a tiny clock radio that she could listen to late-night talk shows. Sometimes, during the process of mopping details Gwen was able to tune her radio to the top 40 stations. It became apparent that the volume on the radio decreased slowly until it would become unlistenable. Gwen could then stroll over to the radio, and then raise it again. Over a time approximately an hour the volume would decrease.

In the course of time, Gwen began to notice that the radio was stop working completely whenever she listened at that Top 40 station, despite being aware that the radio was new. It was returned at home and it was operating perfect. She then plugged it into another boom box, and exactly the same thing took place. But Gwen was able to hear signals as well as "noise" coming from the stereo even when it was turned off and at times even when it was disconnected. Gwen eventually brought the stereo to her home where it functioned perfectly. Although she was a bit agitated, and far from seeking out parapsychologists, Gwen chose not to tune in to the Top 40 radio or any other station whatsoever and all the episodes were stopped.

Within a couple of months of her job in Circle K, Gwen began to feel like she was being observed. Gwen had recently ended dating one of her partners in the moment and admitted to me that she believed that he may be watching her. At times, she was convinced like she was watched by someone just across the street. In one night, she gazed at the outside and saw an unassuming man that appeared to be sitting hunched on a bench in a bus stop in the opposite direction. The man seemed to be gazing right at her. Then, she realized that the man was sitting for around three hours.

Just a few hours prior to dawn it was the time that a policeman arrived for his daily cup of coffee as well as snacks. Gwen requested that she could talk to the gentleman standing across the street as she was uncomfortable about the man's peculiar behaviour. The police officer regarded her in a strange way and then asked "What man?" Gwen was able to see the man who was staring directly in the face turned and said "That man." The officer claimed that he was unable to observe anyone, even though it was obvious for Gwen. He promised that he'd be looking for anyone who was suspicious, and then walked away. Gwen claims that the suspect went missing shortly after the officer had left.

He would appear at times and Gwen attempted to get photos of him or even go out to speak with the guy. In this moment she believed that there was something supernatural going on. The ghostly figure was not recognized by Gwen at all. Yet strange occurrences still went on. The first time it was just some strange sounds, like clicking and bumps. Then it was items falling from shelves, as well as the video game becoming disconnected. It was not long before Gwen became a childsitter for a ghost who was bored. Gwen eventually became comfortable and began calling ghost "George," her dead brother who she believed that the ghost to be.

The milkman arrived with a load. Gwen was at the back of the shop to open the storage space for refrigeration. Gwen was feeling bored, so she chose to talk with the man and assist his unload. She was expecting him to pass through the back but she was surprised by his entrance from the front. The man looked at her bit enviously, and then she asked, "What's the deal with your boss?" Unsure of the topic he was discussing, Gwen responded "What boss?" The milkman said that there was a weird person in an Circle K shirt with a smile that was sour. He then proceeded to refer to the guy as sporting glasses and a hunchback similar to the guy who lives across the street. Gwen almost peed her pants when she heard the news and decided to the counter but found nobody there.

In the following evening, Gwen decided that her hours were over in her Circle K and she gave her notice of two weeks partly due to ghostly conversations, but more importantly due to the fact that she was offered a position in a 7-Eleven store during normal business times. When she was leaving for work the next day the store, she was tired and exhausted around 4:00 am. It was no way she looked at the possibility that she was scheduled to begin her new position that same day at 8:15.

About 4:30 AM an assortment of young youngsters walked into the shop and picked up a range of candy, sodas, as well as nachos. They were seated in the magazines section, eating into their treats. Gwen observed them with care however, she soon fell to sleep. In a matter of minutes she was asleep. Perhaps five minutes later, she was woken by the sound of a paper Nacho boat hitting the floor. The boys were not to be seen as there was an huge messy mess of cheesy food on the floor. Gwen took a look at one of those mirrors with circular shapes to check if they had been involved in any kind plan and saw a shadowy figure in a split second. Gwen headed out to the corridors for a closer look but did not find anyone and found there was nothing.

After a few years of her tenure with Circle K, Gwen ran to her boss from the previous year at the bus stop. The two talked for a while and her boss told her that the shop closed about three months following a massive AM-PM opening and drove the store out of the business. The boss also said that there was no way to keep any one working the graveyard shift. He also said that the manager believed that Gwen did the most work, a total of four months. Also, he said Gwen broke records established by a man who was working prior to her, a tiny and nearsighted man called Jerry who was shot and then killed in a failed burglary just a month prior to when Gwen was hired at the cemetery.

Chapter 9: Coon Hunt

Date received: April 2, 2002

I've published a tale on this site in the past, and was disappointed how it came out. The tale is Apache Hill. While the script wasn't the best, it absolutely true, 100 100% and 100.

The tale I'm about to tell happened to my father. He was a man who I hold absolute respect for, who instructed me not to commit a lie. It was a pet hate of his. He was not a fan of lying, so when he recounted this story to me, I was sure I was hearing the truth. And it was an extremely odd account.

At the age of fifteen years old, Dad used to coon hunt every day and not only for fun but to earn money for fur also. We would've had many unhappy christmases had it not been due to Dad's hunting coons and trapping at the side. In any case, that specific night, he was exploring the road at a ranch named Granite Hills in or very close to Llano, Texas. The hunt lasted for an hour or more, and could observe his hounds following the coon. From the sounds they made, it was a very hot trail also.

He began to move in their direction at which point the hounds ceased to be a hushed. It's not an unusual thing, considering that the hounds do it often for a moment or so, however the duration was longer. The dog's feet soon began falling to the floor as they ran full-speed toward him. They came up the hill with a vengeance, never slowing one bit. They sped all the way to Dad while putting their feet between their legs sprinting in the fastest speed possible straight back to the pickup truck Dad had parked it down the road.

Dad did not move for an entire minute, wondering what it was about. The family had never been through this before. Dad having been Dad was determined to find out more the area, and so he took a walk over the hill and before him was a vast area of dirt that was ripped into pieces, and it appeared to have an enormous pig's torso buried at the center. The man could have walked on to it however at the moment, the temperature dropped and a sound as if somebody was right beside him was heard saying, "Leave now!" The man turned his back and returned to the truck.

As he returned to the vehicle and returned to the truck, he was astonished to discover his hounds at the door of their cages, waiting to greet him, and flapping within their skins. He had been able to catch a coon earlier in the evening and took the decision to apply skin to it prior to leaving. He was about to skin it when a cold blow of wind hit the neck. A voice that sounded similar to the one he was standing next to called, "Get out!"

He swung around with the knife in his hands If anyone was there, their inners could have been the outside. There wasn't anyone there, however Dad sure felt safe and secure. The coon was left in the open, jumped into his vehicle and barreled off from that area. The rancher never returned to the ranch.

I have always thought about why he didn't hunt in the area, but prior to it was my time, I hunted in the area often and brought some huge coons right out of the area. Mom said that she'll remember this as it was the night when he came back from hunting in a clean as a sheet and he didn't talk about it for an extended period of time.

Copy Cat Date of posting in March, 1999

Things I'd like to talk about much more of a short story in essence since they didn't last extremely lengthy. From the time I was small I've witnessed strange happenings in my Dad's and Mom's residence. There's been no actual sighting of ghosts in the house however it's your choice.

A few hours ago, around 2 am I was sleeping when I noticed the hallway lighting come on. I knew my mother was awake which is why I got up, and we started talking. In the hallway I could clearly see the kitchen. The lights were off the kitchen, but I could be able to see through it. I could see my Dad dressed in his uniform in front of me, drinking something. The truth is, my father doesn't start work until around 5:15 AM. I asked my mother, "Why is Daddy up so early?" She looked around and replied, "I don't know," and we entered to turn on the light and saw him gone. Then we went to their room and found that my father was sleeping soundly.

A night, my sister and I had an affair with a man. It was late, and both of my parents are rigorous, so when they observed my dad get up out of bed and walk to the kitchen along with her boyfriend went to hide in the kitchen and waited to see if he would return to bed. Then, he didn't come back in, so my sister went looking in the kitchen but she found him not there.

I was dating an unreliable jerk the time, and my parents were away on holiday. They let us stay at their place and had a sleep in the living room, on the flooring. Both of us folded our clothes carefully before going to bed and awoke up, the clothes of his were scattered everywhere in the house, while mine were neat. He claimed he'd not ever sleep in that house for another night. Maybe the ghost didn't love the ghost too much.

As a teen and my best close friend Danielle lived in our house at a time and shared my bedroom. Our roommate Theresa came over to stay one night, and we lay in our front room, while Danielle was in the room. I'm not a great sleeper and woke up to a bright alarming light that woke me. I stood up to find out the source... It was Danielle at the fridge. What I saw was this ponytail of blonde hair bopping around as if she was looking for something. When I checked the clock, at 3:00 am. I thoughtto myself "Geez, what an oinker," I went back to bed. Next day, I inquired with her about the incident but she told me she had never gotten up. It was then that I thought about the incident. If she had been inside the refrigerator I could have seen the entire body of her as well as her hair due to the way that the fridge is opened. The fridge was open from the other side.

When I was married and left my home, I was a homebody and go to my parents' room when my mother wasn't present in the living room. If she was asleep, I'd walk into the room. My mother always suspected that it was me since footsteps would echo in the home, and she'd awake before I made it into the room. Since I'm no longer there However, in the morning in her absence, she can hear the sound of footsteps. The sound is like somebody's going fast to her bedroom and she's in wait for me to come into the room, but my footsteps cease right before the door. As she stands up and checks to see if she's I, she's not there.

What do you think? Spooky, eh? If they possess a ghost, it won't cause any trouble; it simply assumes the appearance of those in my family. My parents found out in the future that an old lady was killed in our home in the year 1970.

Cult House

Date of receipt: March 1997.

The place that I was raised located in Northern Delaware had the same kind of urban legends, reports and common teenage superstition that I'm sure every community is subject to. As a teenager at high school I heard a particular story that was popular about mansions that were located in the forest of the Brandywine Valley. It was situated located just north of the Pennsylvania frontier. It was referred to as Cult House.

The question is what the reason for this speculation. However, I am aware that some of my buddies' fathers may have a similar tale of the exact location as they were high school students.

According to local lore the mansion is run by the "Satanic Cult." Some versions suggest that it is believed that the "Cult" is associated with an important Delaware family who are involved in the field of chemical. The windows are the form of crossed inverted. The trees that are lining the roads that run on the sides of the home develop at a sharp angle from the home, and in certain locations, far away from the main lighting source. It is interesting to note that there's the "guard house" on the property that is home to the red fleet of pickup trucks. If you pass the property too often and you are not careful, one or more of the trucks might leave the property and pursue you. However close the distance comes, you'll never see the truck driver's face.

There's a particular tree that is located along the highway which runs through the house, which has exposed roots. The roots create the ideal form of the human skull. According to legend, several years ago, police found bones of an sacrificed victim buried in the tree. The reports differ on whether the deceased was a human or an animal. According to legends that a sacrifice of a person takes place at the site every year on Halloween.

It's rumor, at least. Let me share my experience regarding "Cult House." I've been driving through the area with my friends as well as researching the history of the place since around seven years. The windows are formed in the form of crossed inverted cross. The shape isn't always intentional. It could just happen that the specific panes have been designed. Trees do tend to grow at an angle that is quite far from the building and at times tend to separate from the illumination source. The phenomenon ceases when you are about a quarter mile from the home.

There's a security house and red trucks. The trucks have actually been following me previously on two occasions. The first time was late at late at night when the lights of the truck weren't on. Incredible, considering that there are no street lights and the trees permit darkness. I was unable to comprehend why this driver was able to remain in the roadway. I was in the back initially. The truck stopped and waited until I was able to go by. It then left and continued to follow me to a distance of several miles away from my home. We had one other passenger in the car and you can imagine what a state that we were in. The car was a complete nightmare and really thrilled!

Another time, it was after dark, however with a different companion. When we drove by the guardhouse a few times, we realized that we were accompanied by a truck in red. It was the first time we'd seen it arrive on the roadway. We didn't see the driver's face. We were also followed until we had a few miles from home. Then the vehicle pulled off at the end of the highway. The headlights, too, were not working. There has never been a single person leaving or entering the main house, or even at the gatehouse. I'm sure the trucks are located in the guardhouse, as there are always at least five seen from the driveway.

"The "skull tree" does look atrociously like the skull of a person. There are no reports in the newspapers confirming that any remains that were of any sort were discovered within the tree. I've been able to find no evidence of any sacrificial rituals taking place in the Halloween season or other times, as per local reports.

A couple of other mysterious things that are associated with the home. For starters, the road that passes by the property is not listed found on any map I've ever looked at, and it's true that I've seen maps. Two roads "Cult House Road" connects are shown on the map however the road itself is not. It is not marked with a street marker that indicates its location. It is considered a public street because there are road signs, but it does not belong to the land of the home situated about a quarter of a mile away of the street. County records offices cannot provide no titles for an area which matches the property description.

The paper in the area decided to do an Halloween-themed feature about the myth, hoping to bring information and cutting some congestion on the rural roads. The editor for the city desk of the newspaper, one of my friends, stated that the paper found a number for the home somehow, and they called to arrange an interview. They said they wanted to "debunk" the legend once and once and for all. The woman said that they were rudely denied by a man who refused to even reveal his name. The staff of the paper was shocked as they thought the owner would be looking to end the gossip.

In the final part, I'd like provide some personal opinions about the property. We're not able to guarantee all the information about the home is accurate. You can only trust my personal observations. It definitely has an oppressive vibe. A number of my colleagues are in the midst of panic simply being around it. There was a girl I know who thought she was at risk of being possessed because she was close to the home. The spirit that she saw was a female victim of ritual carried out on the areas. The woman denied having any previous information about the mythology that surround the home.

Sometimes, I've believed I've observed people walking through the trees that surround the home. If I check again I see them away. I've been chased down the road in front of their guards. My family as well as I have witnessed animals roaming in the forest and along the roads that we are unable to recognize. It could have nothing to do with have anything to do with our house However, it definitely adds to that "weirdness" of the environment. I'm not sure how to describe it in a proper way when you've walked towards Cult House road, you are like you're in another world. Everything feels different.

www.ingramcontent.com/pod-product-compliance
Lightning Source LLC
Chambersburg PA
CBHW070555010526
44118CB00012B/1326